HARCOURT SCHOOL PUBLISHERS
STORYtown

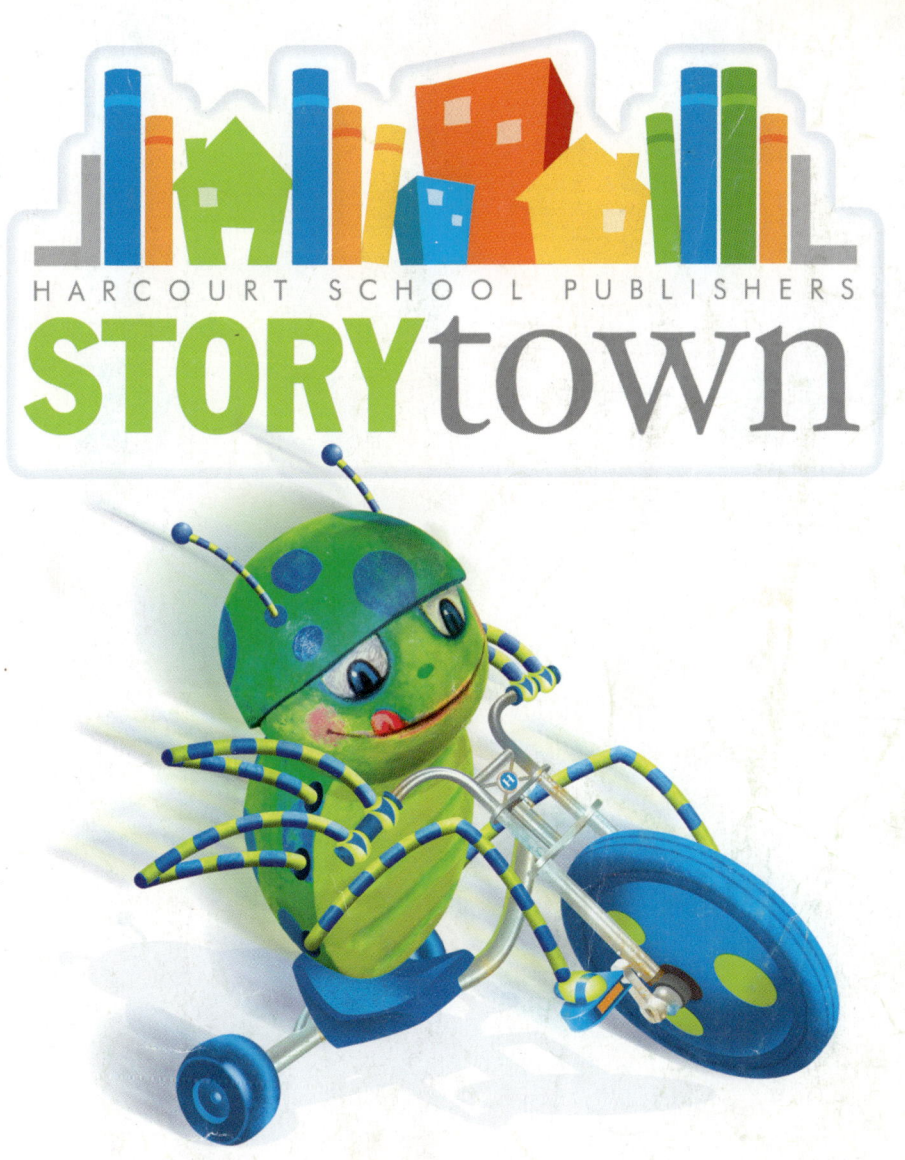

Zoom Along

Senior Authors
Isabel L. Beck • Roger C. Farr • Dorothy S. Strickland

Authors
Alma Flor Ada • Roxanne F. Hudson • Margaret G. McKeown
Robin C. Scarcella • Julie A. Washington

Consultants
F. Isabel Campoy • Tyrone C. Howard • David A. Monti

Harcourt
SCHOOL PUBLISHERS

www.harcourtschool.com

Copyright © 2008 by Harcourt, Inc.

All rights reserved. No part of this publication may be reproduced or transmitted in any form or by any means, electronic or mechanical, including photocopy, recording, or any information storage and retrieval system, without permission in writing from the publisher.

Requests for permission to make copies of any part of the work should be addressed to School Permissions and Copyrights, Harcourt, Inc., 6277 Sea Harbor Drive, Orlando, Florida 32887-6777. Fax: 407-345-2418.

STORYTOWN is a trademark of Harcourt, Inc. HARCOURT and the Harcourt Logo are trademarks of Harcourt, Inc. registered in the United States of America and/or other jurisdictions.

Printed in the United States of America

ISBN 10 0-15-369859-4
ISBN 13 978-0-15-369859-0

If you have received these materials as examination copies free of charge, Harcourt School Publishers retains title to the materials and they may not be resold. Resale of examination copies is strictly prohibited and is illegal.

Possession of this publication in print format does not entitle users to convert this publication, or any portion of it, into electronic format.

2 3 4 5 6 7 8 9 10 751 16 15 14 13 12 11 10 09 08

STORYtown
HARCOURT SCHOOL PUBLISHERS

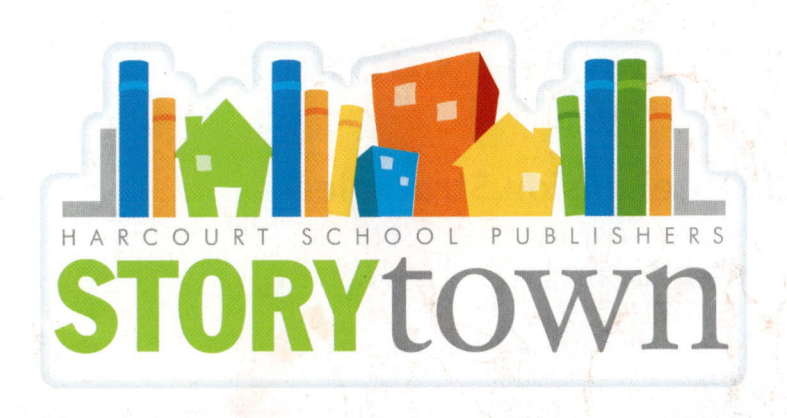

Zoom Along

Harcourt
SCHOOL PUBLISHERS

www.harcourtschool.com

Theme 3
Turning Corners

Contents

Comprehension Strategies 8

Theme Opener 12

Lesson 7

Social Studies

Get Started Story

Ten Eggs 16
Phonics: Short Vowel e 24
Words to Know 26

Little Red Hen Gets Help 28
by Kenneth Spengler • illustrated by Margaret Spengler • FANTASY

Paired Selections

Let's Make Tortillas! 46
RECIPE

Social Studies

Connections 48

Theme Writing — Reading-Writing Connection 50
Student Writing Model: Describing an Event

4

Lesson 8

Get Started Story

Thanks, Seth! 54
Details 62
Words to Know 64

Beth's Job 66
by Carole Roberts • illustrated by Michael Garland • REALISTIC FICTION

Flowers Grow 88
NONFICTION

Connections 90

Lesson 9

Get Started Story

A Nut Falls 94
Details 102
Words to Know 104

Plants Can't Jump 106
by Ned Crowley • NONFICTION

Cornfield Leaves 128
by Lessie Jones Little • POETRY

Connections 130

5

Lesson 10

Get Started Story

Frog Gets His Song 134

Social Studies

Plot 142

Words to Know 144

Soccer Song 146
by Patricia Reilly Giff • illustrated by Blanche Sims • REALISTIC FICTION

Now You Know About Soccer 164
NONFICTION

Paired Selections

Social Studies

Connections 166

Lesson 11

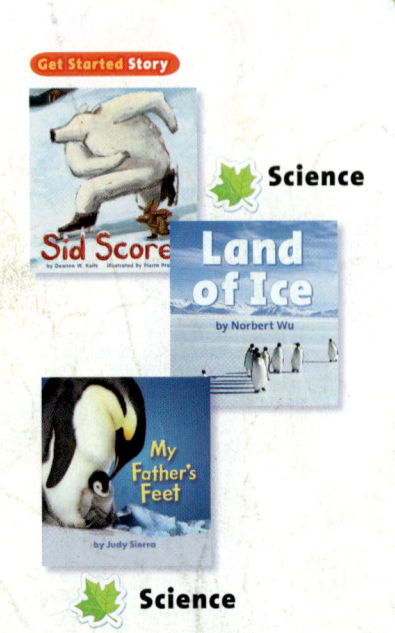

Get Started Story

Sid Scores 170

Science

Words with or and ore 178

Words to Know 180

Land of Ice 182
by Norbert Wu • NONFICTION

Paired Selections

My Father's Feet 204
by Judy Sierra • POETRY

Science

Connections 206

6

Lesson 12

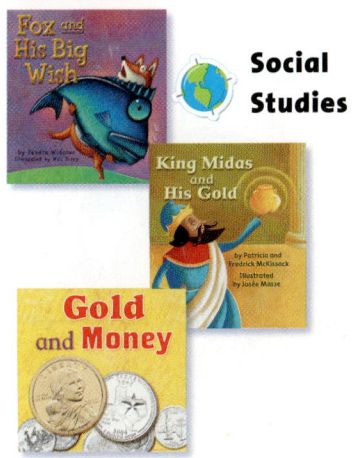

Get Started Story

Fox and His Big Wish 210

Setting 218

Words to Know 220

King Midas and His Gold 222

by Patricia and Fredrick McKissack • illustrated by Josée Masse • MYTH

Paired Selections

Gold and Money 244

NONFICTION

Connections 246

Glossary 248

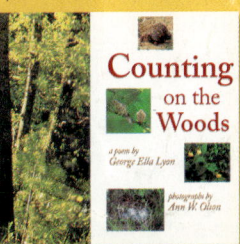

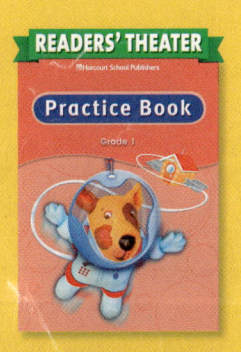

Social Studies

Social Studies

Theme Big Books

Decodable Books 7–12

"The Frog and the Ox"

Comprehension Strategies

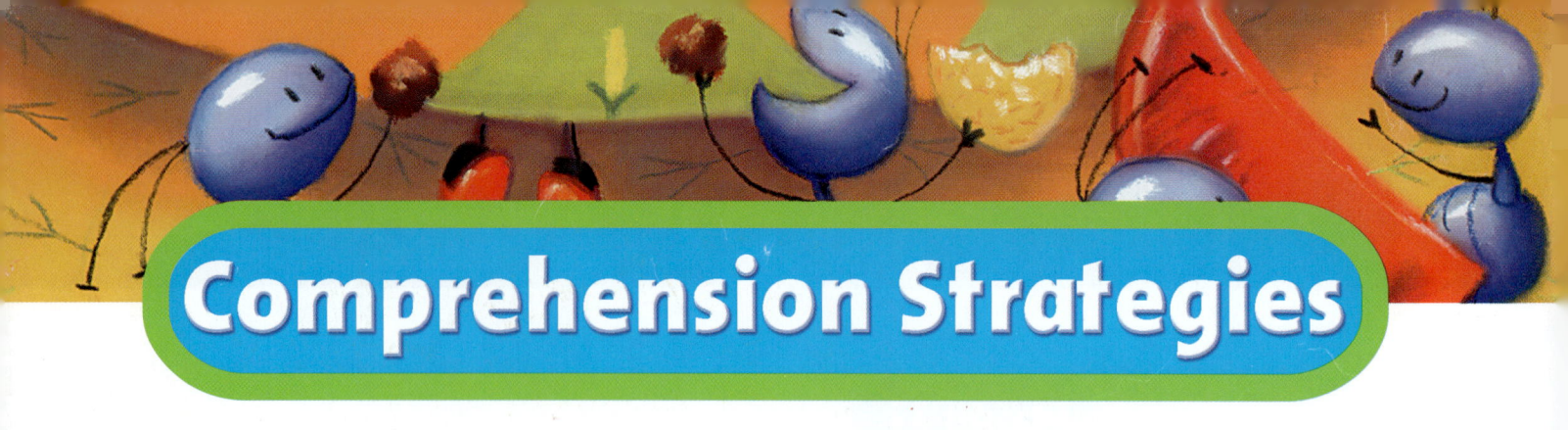

Before You Read

Look at the pictures. Think about what you already know.

Set a purpose.

I want to find out about frogs.

While You Read

Ask questions.

What do frogs eat?

Reread.

I'll read this page again.

Answer questions.

Oh! Some frogs eat bugs.

After You Read

Summarize.

First, tadpoles hatch from eggs. Then, they begin changing into frogs. Last, they are full-grown frogs.

Make connections.

This is like another book I read. I learned about how butterflies change.

READING-WRITING CONNECTION

	Lesson 7	**Lesson 8**	**Lesson 9**
Selection Titles	Ten Eggs Little Red Hen Gets Help Let's Make Tortillas!	Thanks, Seth! Beth's Job Flowers Grow	A Nut Falls Plants Can't Jump Cornfield Leaves
Comprehension Strategies	Answer Questions	Use Graphic Organizers	Reading Rate
Focus Skills	Short Vowel e	Details	Details

12

Theme 3 Turning Corners

The Gardeners, Judy Byford

Lesson 10
Frog Gets His Song
Soccer Song
Now You Know About Soccer

Recognize Story Structure

Plot

Lesson 11
Sid Scores
Land of Ice
My Father's Feet

Make Inferences

Words with <u>or</u> and <u>ore</u>

Lesson 12
Fox and His Big Wish
King Midas and His Gold
Gold and Money

Ask Questions

Setting

13

Contents

Get Started Story

"Ten Eggs" 16
by Nancy Furstinger • illustrated by Lori Lohstoeter

Read this Get Started Story.

Short Vowel e 24
Learn to read words with short vowel e.

Words to Know 26
Learn to read and write new high-frequency words.

"Little Red Hen Gets Help" 28
by Kenneth Spengler • illustrated by Margaret Spengler

- Learn the features of fantasy.
- Learn to find answers to questions while reading.

"Let's Make Tortillas!" 46
Learn how to make tortillas.

Connections 48
- Compare texts.
- Write about helping.
- Practice building words.
- Reread for fluency.

Lesson 7

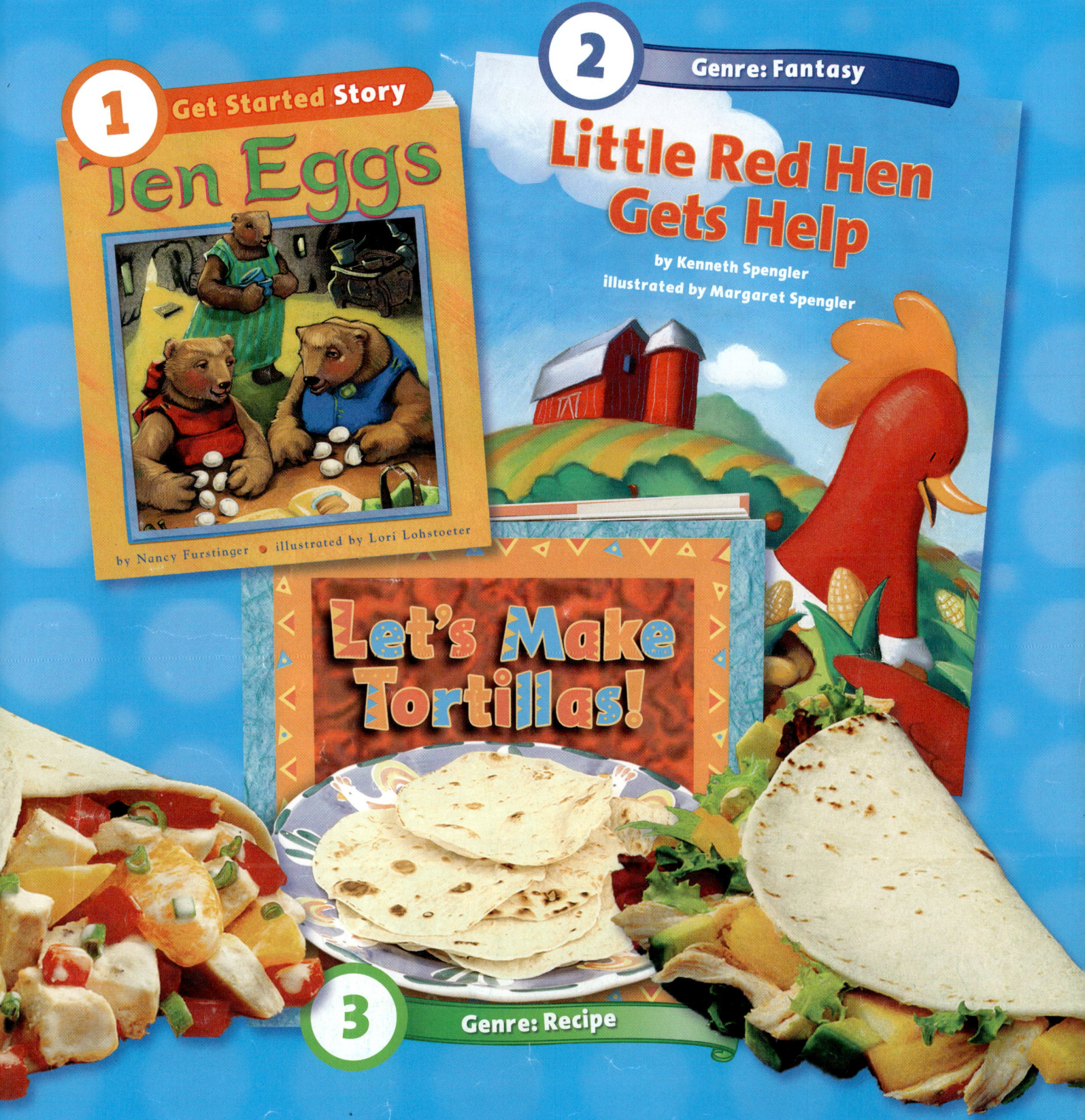

1 Get Started Story
Ten Eggs
by Nancy Furstinger • illustrated by Lori Lohstoeter

2 Genre: Fantasy
Little Red Hen Gets Help
by Kenneth Spengler
illustrated by Margaret Spengler

Let's Make Tortillas!

3 Genre: Recipe

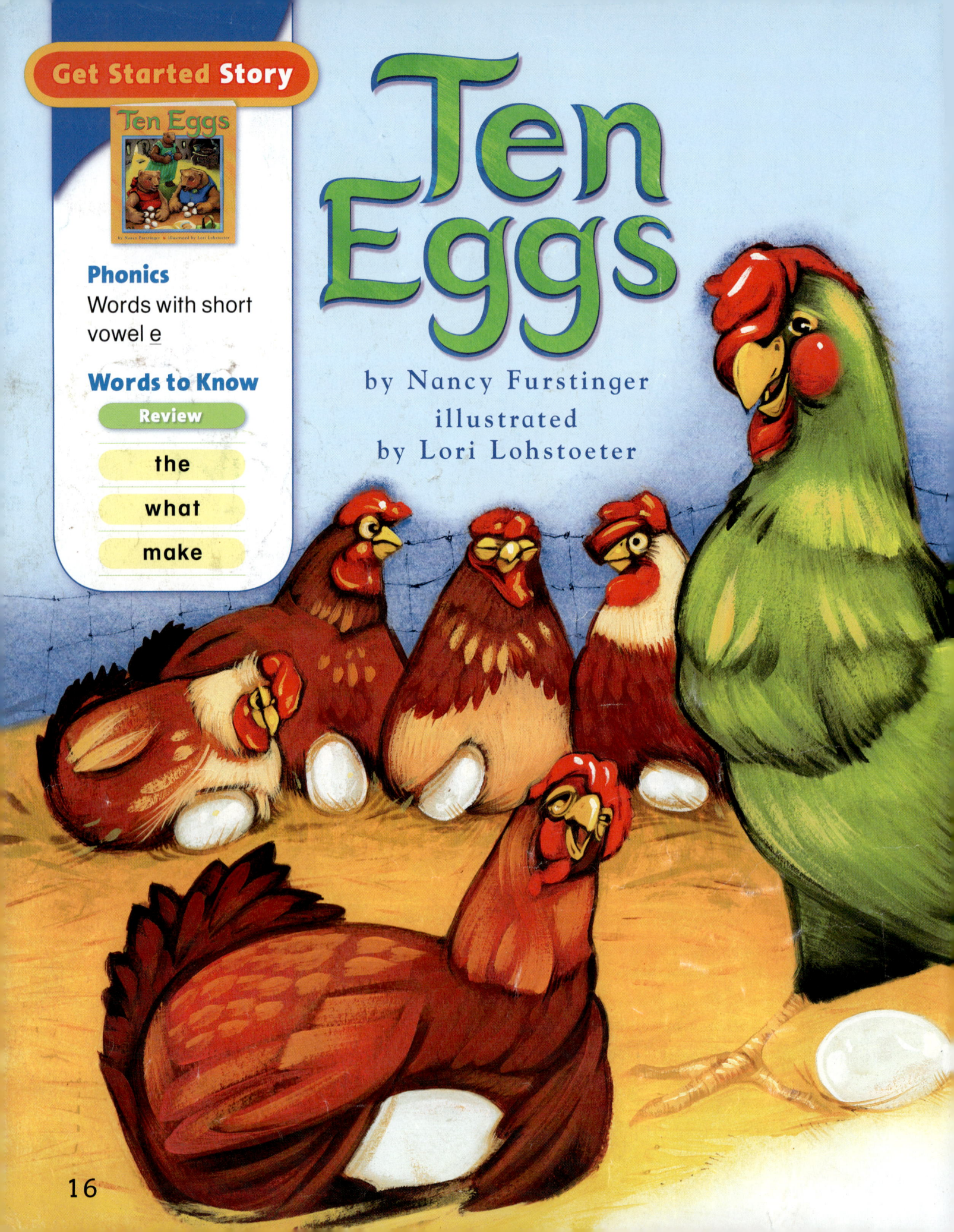

Get Started Story

Phonics
Words with short vowel e

Words to Know

Review
- the
- what
- make

Ten Eggs

by Nancy Furstinger
illustrated by Lori Lohstoeter

Ten hens had ten eggs.

Jen got six eggs.
Ken got the rest.

18

Jen mixed the eggs.
Ken mixed the eggs.

What a big mess!

Did Jen and Ken get help?

Yes! Mom got a pan.
In went the eggs.

What did Mom make?
The best eggs yet!

23

Phonics Skill

Short Vowel e

The letter **e** can stand for the sound at the beginning of the words **egg** and **elephant**.

egg   elephant

The letter **e** can stand for the sound in the middle of the words **pen** and **net**.

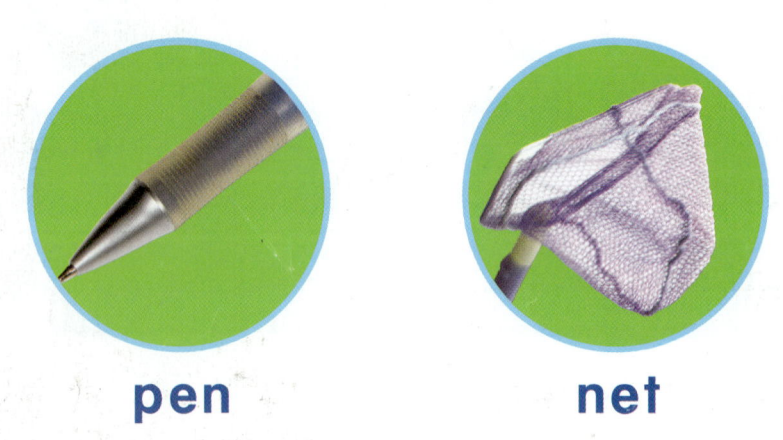

pen   net

Look at each picture. Read the words. Tell which word names the picture.

ten

hen

him

vent

vat

vest

www.harcourtschool.com/storytown

Try This!

Read the sentences.

I have a pet.

He is called Jet.

He went to the vet.

Now he can rest.

OKLAHOMA PASS—1RL3.1 decode one-syllable words; 1RL3.1a decode using short/long vowel patterns

Words to Know

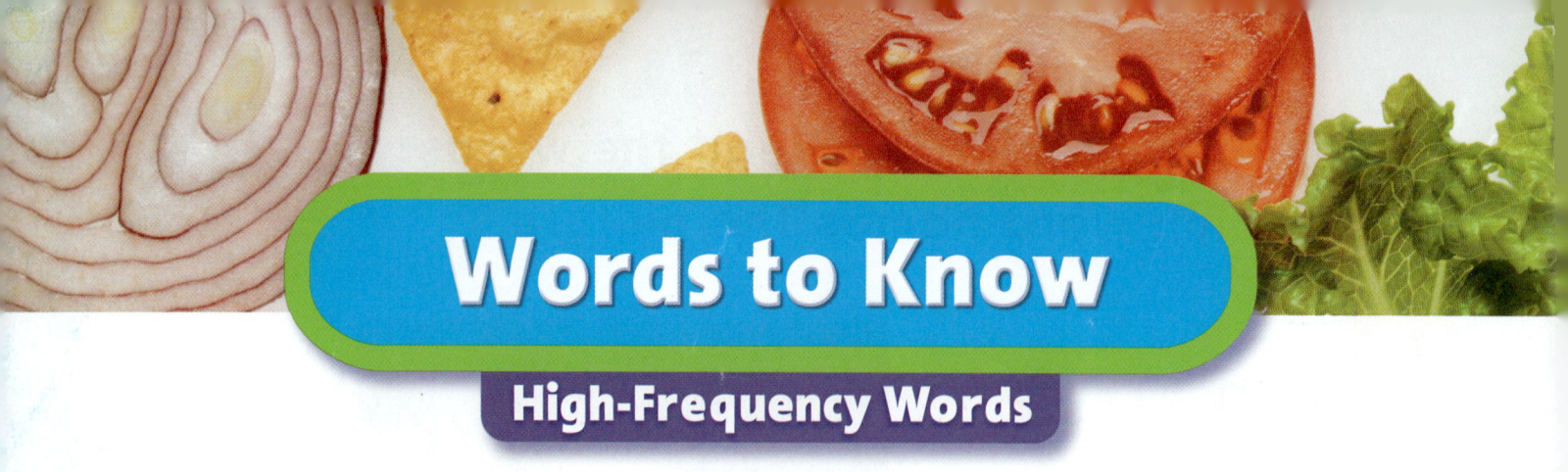

High-Frequency Words

- day
- said
- eat
- first
- time
- was

"It is a hot **day**," **said** Hen.

"Let's **eat**," said Cat.

"**First** add some of this," said Fox.

"Now it is **time** to add this," said Pig.

"That **was** fast!" said Hen.

www.harcourtschool.com/storytown

Award Winner

Little Red Hen Gets Help
by Kenneth Spengler
Illustrated by Margaret Spengler

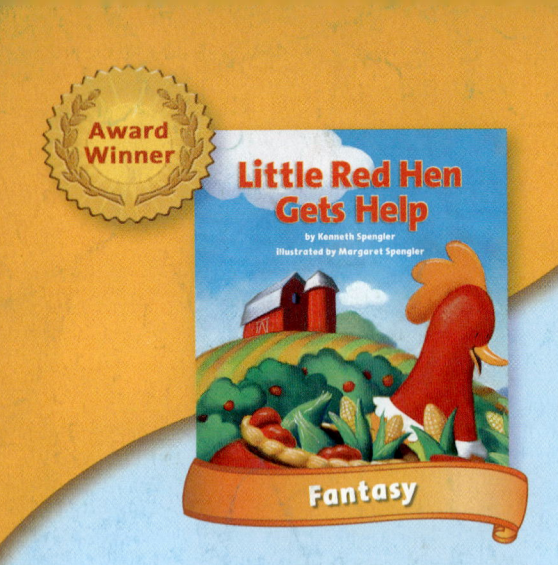

Fantasy

1RL7.1
1RL7.1a

Genre Study

A **fantasy** is a made-up story. The events could never really happen.

What Little Red Hen Asks	What the Characters Say and Do

1RL6.1c

Comprehension Strategy

Answer Questions To answer questions about the story, think about the words you read. Use what you already know to figure out answers, too.

OKLAHOMA PASS—1RL6.1c respond to questions; 1RL7.1 know/ appreciate various genres; 1RL7.1a discriminate between fiction/nonfiction

Little Red Hen Gets Help

by Kenneth Spengler
illustrated by Margaret Spengler

One day, Little Red Hen got up.
She was hungry.

"Who wants to eat this?" she asked.

"Not I," said Cat.
"I can't," said Fox.
"Oh, no," said Pig.

"Who wants tacos?" asked Red Hen.

"I do!" they all yelled.

"Will you help make some tacos?"

"Yes!" said Cat.
"I will!" said Fox.
"Let me, too!" said Pig.

37

Red Hen fed Cat, Fox, and Pig.

"What a mess! Who will pick up?"

"Not I," said Cat.
"I can't," said Fox.
"Oh, no," said Pig.

"We will help!" called the ants.

"Thank you, ants" said Red Hen.
"Next time, I will ask you first!"

Think Critically

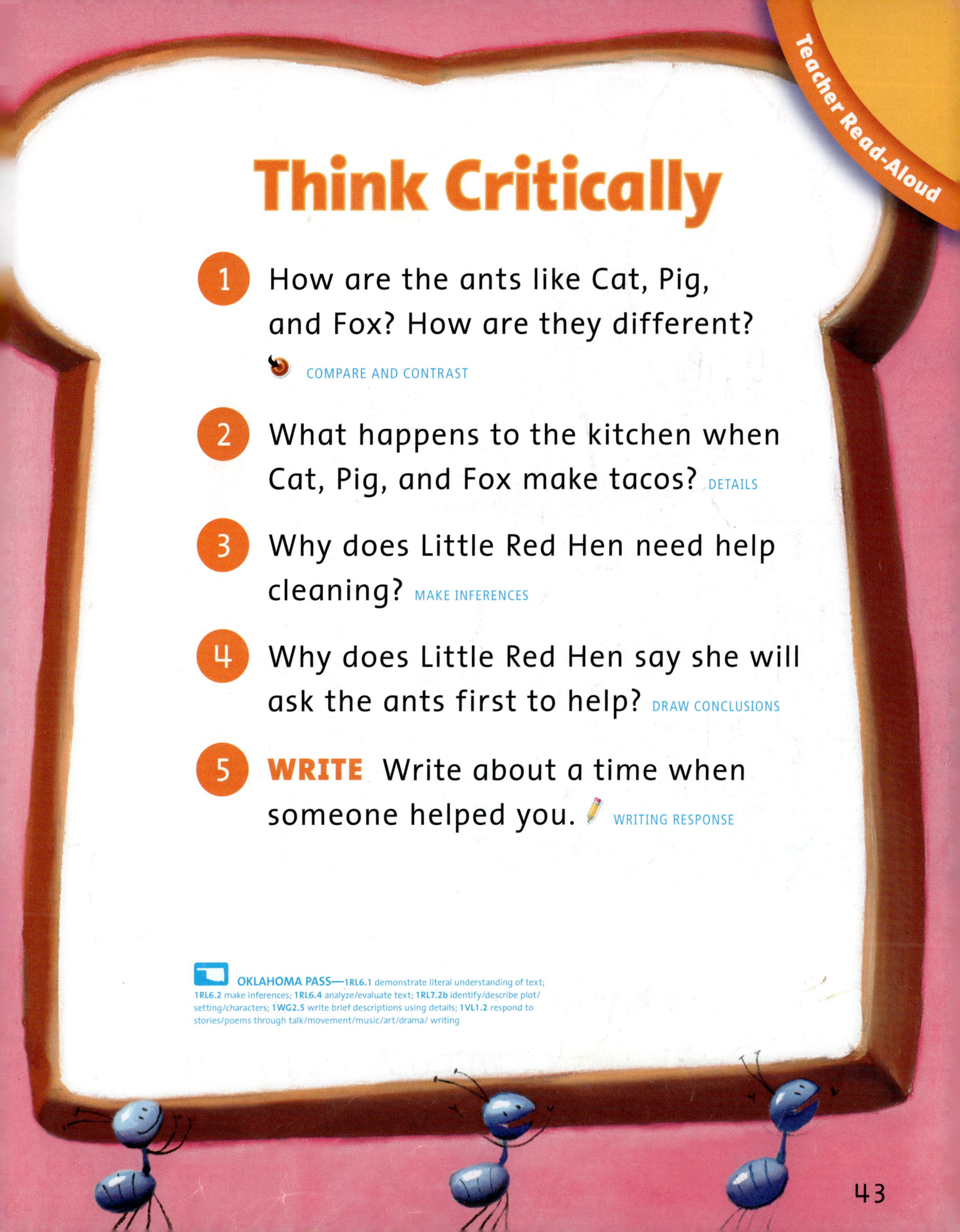

1 How are the ants like Cat, Pig, and Fox? How are they different? **COMPARE AND CONTRAST**

2 What happens to the kitchen when Cat, Pig, and Fox make tacos? **DETAILS**

3 Why does Little Red Hen need help cleaning? **MAKE INFERENCES**

4 Why does Little Red Hen say she will ask the ants first to help? **DRAW CONCLUSIONS**

5 **WRITE** Write about a time when someone helped you. **WRITING RESPONSE**

OKLAHOMA PASS—**1RL6.1** demonstrate literal understanding of text; **1RL6.2** make inferences; **1RL6.4** analyze/evaluate text; **1RL7.2b** identify/describe plot/setting/characters; **1WG2.5** write brief descriptions using details; **1VL1.2** respond to stories/poems through talk/movement/music/art/drama/writing

Teacher Read-Aloud

Meet the Author
Kenneth Spengler

Kenneth Spengler likes to write funny stories. He worked with his wife, Margaret, on this one.

"I liked writing this story because I love food, especially tacos! Just like the Little Red Hen, I like help when I cook. Sometimes we spill food on the floor. Our dog, Jackie, helps clean it up, though, not ants!"

Meet the Illustrator
Margaret Spengler

Margaret Spengler is the artist who made the pictures for this story. She painted them on sand paper with pastel chalk and water. The thing she likes best about being an artist is being creative.

"I like the Little Red Hen because she is smart and caring. I also like the way she shares with her friends."

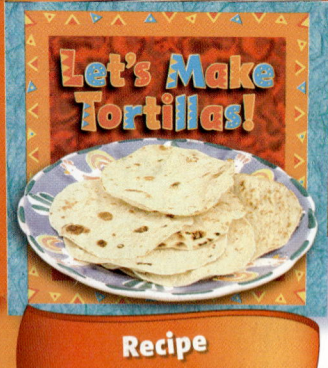

Social Studies

Recipe

Teacher Read-Aloud

Let's Make Tortillas!

1½ cups flour

½ teaspoon salt

2 tablespoons oil

½ cup warm water

1 **Mix** the flour, salt, oil, and water.

2 Roll six balls.
Make six circles.

3 Cook in a pan.

4 Eat the tortillas!
You can fill them
to make tacos.

Teacher Read-Aloud

Connections

Comparing Texts 1RL6.1c 1RL6.2 1RL7.1

❶ What did you find out about making tacos from the story? What did you learn from the recipe?

❷ How do you help clean up at home?

❸ Which of Little Red Hen's jobs would you do best? Tell why.

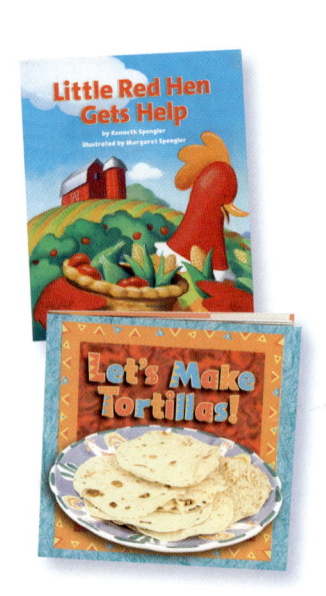

Writing 1WG2 1VL1.2

Imagine that you are in the story. Write about how you would help.

What Little Red Hen Asks	How I Would Help

48

Phonics

Make and read new words.

Start with **egg**.

Add [l] in front of [e]. Take off [g].

Change [g] to [t].

Change [l] to [w].

Add [n] after [e].

Fluency Practice

Work with a small group. Decide who will be each animal in "Little Red Hen Gets Help." Read the story. Use your voice to show how your character feels. Look at the end marks of sentences to help you.

I will!

Yes!

Let me, too!

Teacher Read-Aloud

Reading-Writing Connection

Describing an Event

"Little Red Hen Gets Help" is about something that Little Red Hen and her friends did. After we read the story, we wrote about something that we did.

▶ **First, we talked about the story.**

▶ **Next, we talked about things we have done. We made up sentences to tell about an event.**

▶ **Last, we read our sentences.**

Our class went to the zoo. We saw lions, bears, and many other animals. We ate lunch at the zoo, and then we came home. We all had a great time!

Contents

Get Started Story

"Thanks, Seth!" 54
by Anne Mansk • illustrated by Linda Bronson

Read this Get Started Story.

Details 62
Learn to look for details in a story.

Words to Know 64
Learn to read and write new high-frequency words.

"Beth's Job" 66
by Carole Roberts • illustrated by Michael Garland

- Learn the features of realistic fiction.
- Learn how to use graphic organizers.

"Flowers Grow" 88
Learn how a seed becomes a flower.

Connections 90
- Compare texts.
- Write a question and an answer.
- Practice building words.
- Reread for fluency.

Lesson 8

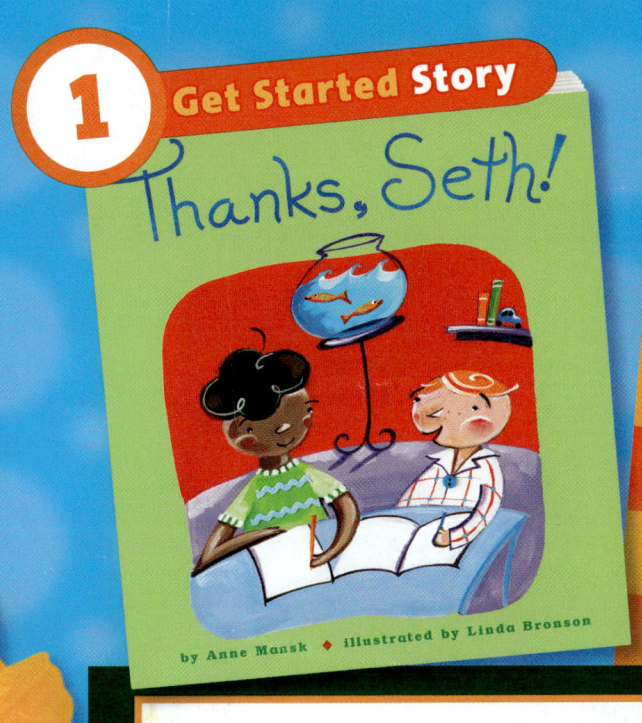

1 Get Started Story

Thanks, Seth!
by Anne Mansk • illustrated by Linda Bronson

2 Genre: Realistic Fiction

Beth's Job
by Carole Roberts
illustrated by Michael Garland

3
Flowers Grow
Genre: Nonfiction

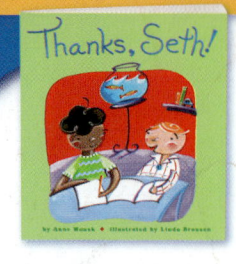

Get Started Story

Phonics
Words with th

Words to Know
Review
- do
- sees
- he
- the
- now

Thanks, Seth!

by Anne Mansk
illustrated by Linda Bronson

Ben is not glad.
"Can I do this math?"

Seth sees Ben.
"I can help Ben," thinks Seth.

Ben sees Seth.
Seth tells Ben he can help.

Seth helps Ben with the task.

Now Ben can add fast.

Seth and Ben are glad!
Ben did all the math.

Thanks, Seth!

Focus Skill

Details

Details give small bits of information about something. Details help you picture the person, animal, place, or thing in your mind.

Look at the picture.

It shows details of what this child is having for lunch.

Tell about this picture. What details do you see?

Try This!

Look at the picture. Tell how the details help you understand what is happening.

www.harcourtschool.com/storytown

OKLAHOMA PASS—1RL6 build comprehension/develop critical literacy

Words to Know

High-Frequency Words

- don't
- says
- water
- Mr.
- new
- line
- her

"I **don't** have a job," **says** Beth.

"You can **water** this plant," **Mr.** Hall says.

Max has a **new** job, too.

He helps Hops.

We get in **line** to pet **her**.

www.harcourtschool.com/storytown

OKLAHOMA PASS—1RL5.4 recognize high-frequency/common irregularly spelled words

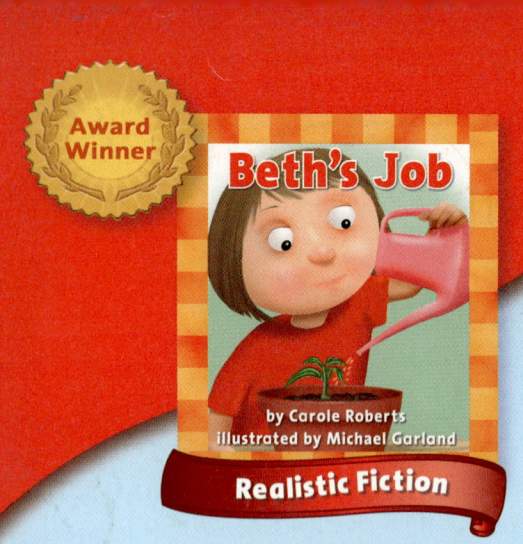

Award Winner

Beth's Job
by Carole Roberts
illustrated by Michael Garland
Realistic Fiction

1RL7.1
1RL7.1a
Genre Study
Realistic fiction stories are made up, but they could happen in real life.

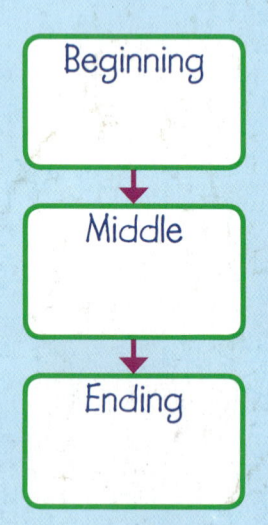

- Beginning
- Middle
- Ending

1RL8.1d
Comprehension Strategy
Use Graphic Organizers A story map can help you understand and remember the beginning, middle, and ending of a story.

OKLAHOMA PASS—1RL7.1 know/appreciate various genres; 1RL7.1a discriminate between fiction/nonfiction; 1RL8.1d access information from charts/maps/graphs/calendars

Beth's Job

by Carole Roberts
illustrated by Michael Garland

It's the day for new jobs.

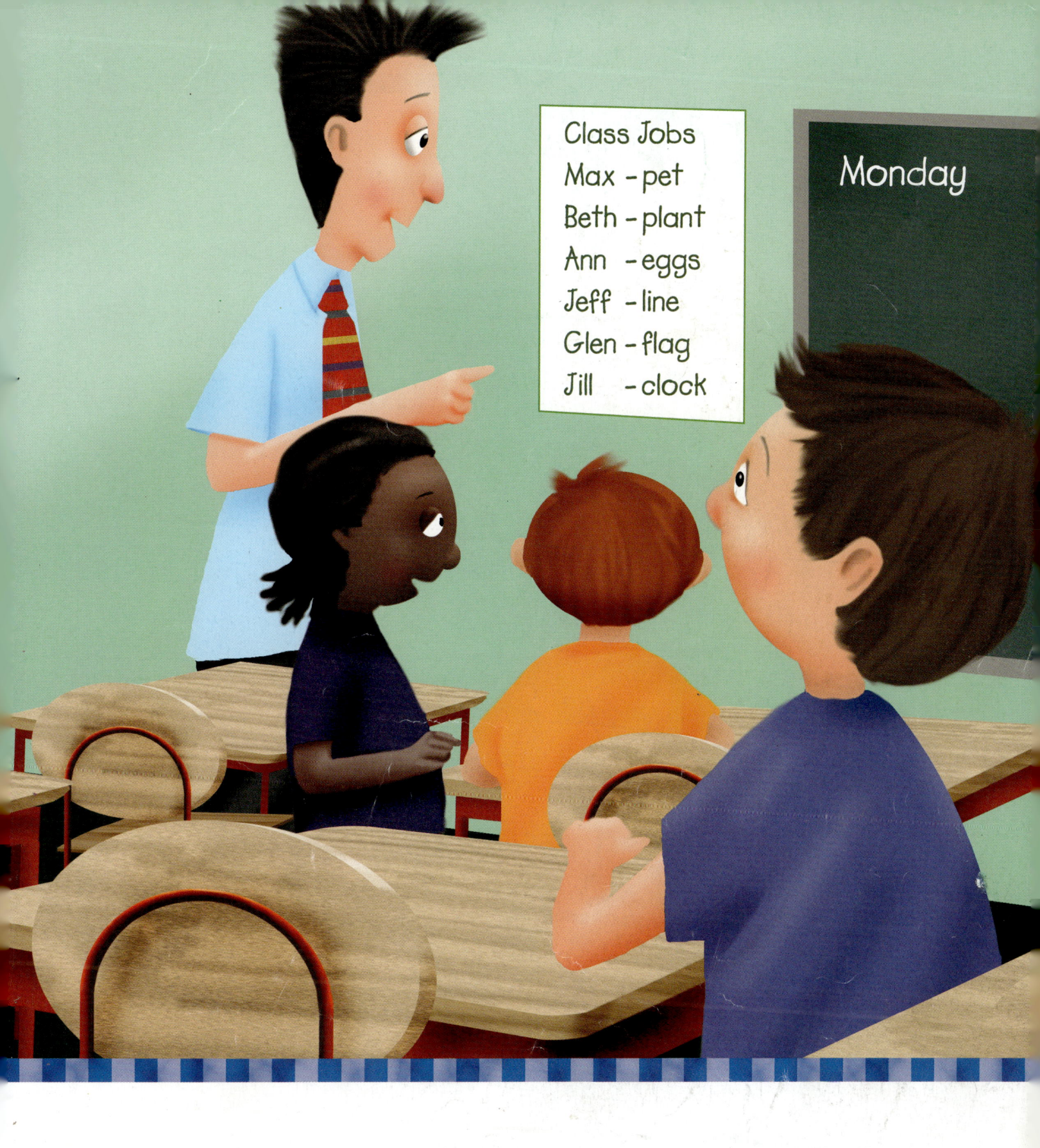

Class Jobs
Max - pet
Beth - plant
Ann - eggs
Jeff - line
Glen - flag
Jill - clock

Monday

"What is my job?" asks Beth.

"You can water the plant," says Mr. Hall.

Class Jobs
Max - pet
Beth - plant
Ann - eggs
Jeff - line
Glen - flag
Jill -

Monday

"Oh, no," thinks Beth.

Max helps with Hops.
Hops is the class pet.

"I want that job," thinks Beth.

Ann helps with the eggs.

Beth wants that job.

Jeff is first in line.

Beth wants that job, too.

77

Glen gets to hold the flag.

"I want to hold the flag," thinks Beth.

"I don't like this plant," thinks Beth.

"I want a new job."

"Look at this flower, Beth!" says Mr. Hall.

"Oh, my!" says the class.

"Oh, my!" says Beth.
"How did that get there?"

"This job is the best!"
Beth likes her job at last!

Think Critically

1 How does Beth feel about her job when the story begins? How does she feel at the end? Why?

COMPARE AND CONTRAST

2 What is one thing Beth does to help the plant? DETAILS

3 Why do you think Beth wants to help with the eggs? MAKE INFERENCES

4 How does Beth's job make the classroom a better place?

DRAW CONCLUSIONS

5 **WRITE** Write about a job you enjoy doing. Tell why that job is important. WRITING RESPONSE

OKLAHOMA PASS—1RL6.1 demonstrate literal understanding of text; 1RL6.2 make inferences; 1RL6.4 analyze/evaluate text; 1RL7.2b identify/describe plot/setting/characters; 1WG2.5 write brief descriptions using details; 1VL1.2 respond to stories/poems through talk/movement/music/art/drama/ writing

Meet the Illustrator
Michael Garland

Michael Garland has written and illustrated many books for children. He spent his childhood in New York exploring the woods, playing sports, and drawing. Drawing was the thing he did best. When he would draw something in school, his teachers would often show it to the class and put it up on the bulletin board. This helped him to decide he wanted to become an artist.

www.harcourtschool.com/storytown

Science

Flowers Grow
Nonfiction

Teacher Read-Aloud

Flowers Grow

A plant needs water, light, air, and soil to grow.

seed

seedling

young plant

bud

flower

The plant grows.

Now there is a flower.
How nice!

89

Teacher Read-Aloud

Connections

Comparing Texts   1RL6.1c 1RL6.4 1RL6.2 1RL7

1. How is the plant in "Beth's Job" like the one in "Flowers Grow"?

2. How is Beth's classroom like your classroom? How is it different?

3. Tell about a job you have had at school.

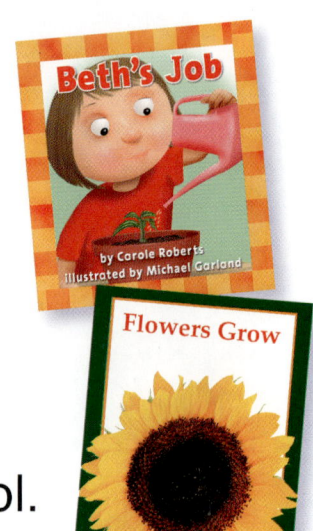

Writing   1RL6.3c 1WG2.1 1VL1.2

Draw three pictures to show how Beth feels at the beginning, middle, and end of the story. Label each picture with a word or sentence.

Beth is sad because she doesn't like her job.

90

Phonics   1RL3.1 1RL3.1c

Make and read new words.

Start with **path**.

Take away **pa**. Add **in** after **th**.

Change **i** to **a**.

Add **k** to the end.

Fluency Practice   1RL5.2 1RL5.4 1RL5.3 1RL5.5

Read the story aloud with a small group. Look at the end marks of the sentences as you read. Use your voice to show how Beth and her classmates feel.

OKLAHOMA PASS—1RL3.1 decode one-syllable words; 1RL3.1c decode using blends/digraphs/diphthongs; 1RL5.2 read instructional-level text; 1RL5.3 engage in repeated readings to increase fluency; 1RL5.4 recognize high-frequency/common irregularly spelled words; 1RL5.5 use punctuation cues to understand meaning; 1RL6.1c respond to questions; 1RL6.2 make inferences; 1RL6.3c draw/discuss visual images; 1RL6.4 analyze/evaluate text; 1RL7 read/respond to a variety of literary forms; 1WG2.1 develop descriptive/expository/narrative stories; 1VL1.2 respond to stories/poems through talk/movement/music/art/drama/ writing

Contents

Get Started Story

"A Nut Falls" 94

by Sandra Widener • illustrated by Doug Bowles

Read this Get Started Story.

Details 102

Practice looking for details in a nonfiction selection.

Words to Know 104

Learn to read and write new high-frequency words.

"Plants Can't Jump" 106

by Ned Crowley

- Learn the features of nonfiction.
- Learn how to read quickly or slowly when I need to.

"Cornfield Leaves" 128

Listen to a poem about plants by Lessie Jones Little.

Connections 130

- Compare texts.
- Draw a picture of a plant and label the parts.
- Practice building words.
- Reread for fluency.

Lesson 9

1 Get Started Story

A Nut Falls
by Sandra Widener
illustrated by Doug Bowles

2 Genre: Nonfiction

Plants Can't Jump
by Ned Crowley

3 Genre: Poetry

Cornfield Leaves
by Lessie Jones Little
illustrated by Don Tate

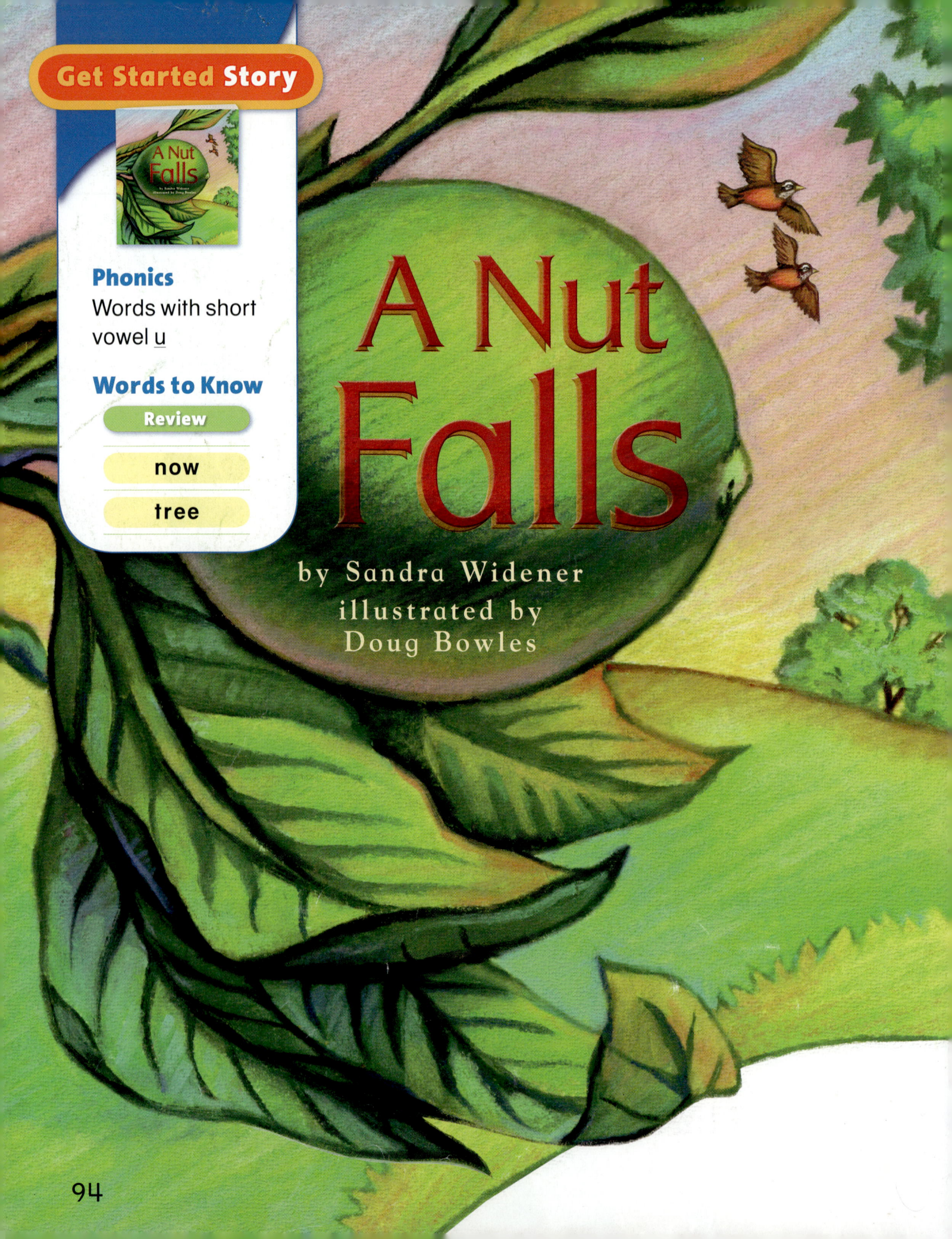

Get Started Story

Phonics
Words with short vowel u

Words to Know
Review
now
tree

A Nut Falls

by Sandra Widener
illustrated by Doug Bowles

Thud! A nut falls in mud.

Sun falls on that nut.
Next that nut gets wet.

The stem pops up!
That nut is now a small plant.

The plant is tall.
It is a big nut tree!

Small buds are on that tree.
Small nuts are on that tree.

Small nuts get big.
Men pick nuts off the tree.

A nut fell in mud.
That nut is now a big tree!

Focus Skill

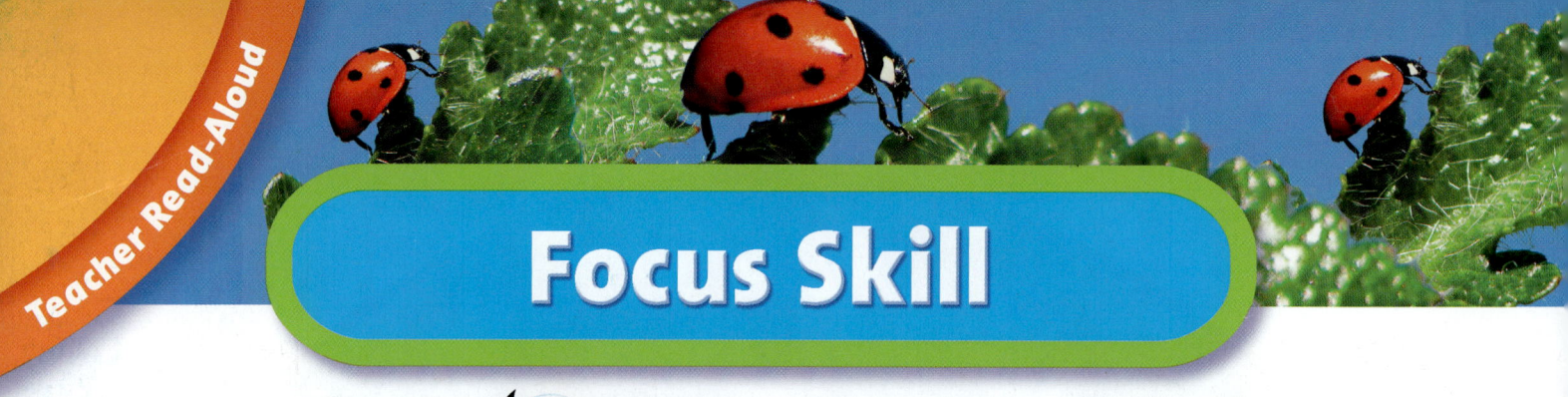

Details

Details give small bits of information about something. Details can tell what something looks like, how it sounds, or what it does.

Look at the picture.

The artist is drawing details he sees in the real flower.

Tell about this picture. What details do you see?

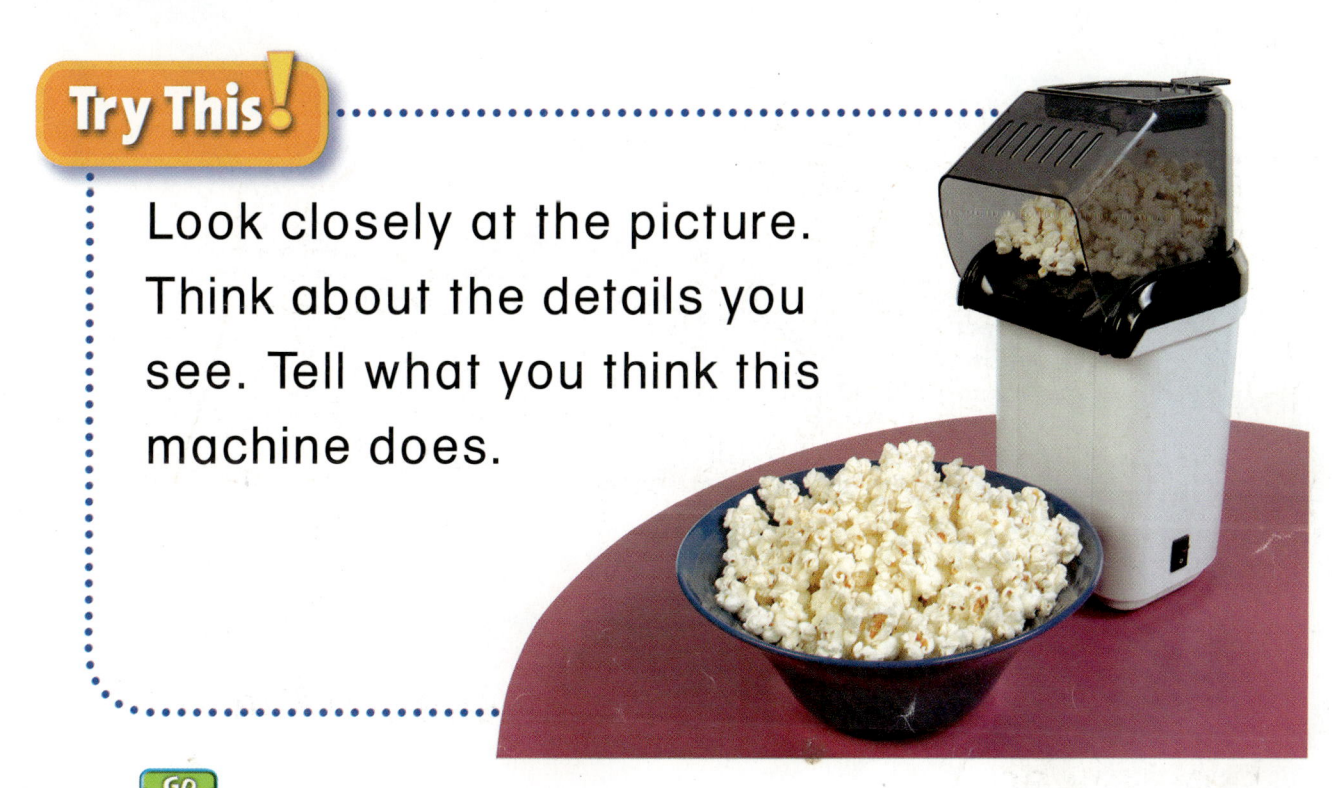

Try This!

Look closely at the picture. Think about the details you see. Tell what you think this machine does.

www.harcourtschool.com/storytown

OKLAHOMA PASS—1RL6 build comprehension/develop critical literacy

103

Words to Know

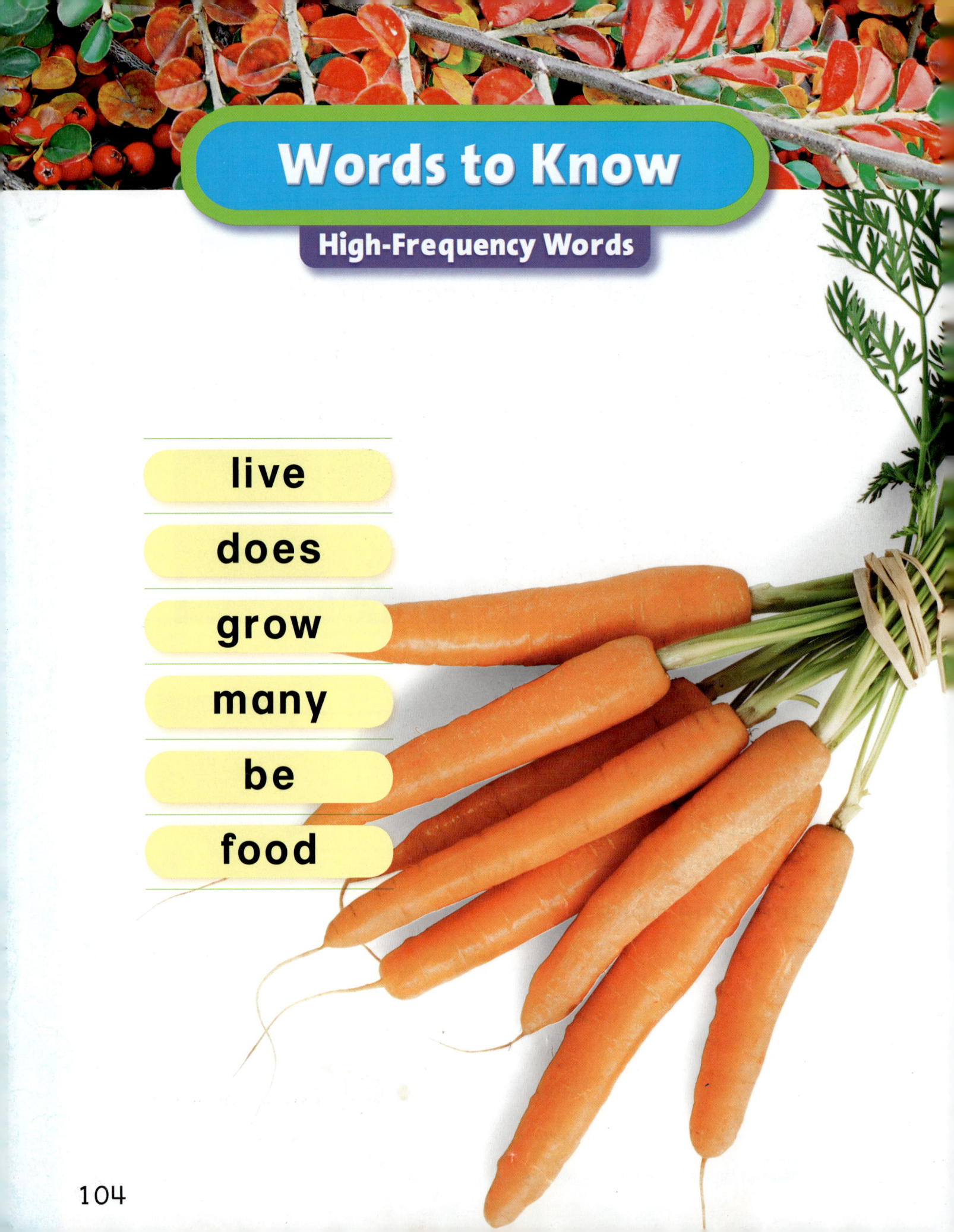

High-Frequency Words

- live
- does
- grow
- many
- be
- food

Where can a plant **live**?

Where **does** it **grow**?

Many plants can **be food**.

Many can grow flowers.

www.harcourtschool.com/storytown

1RL7.1
1RL7.1a

Genre Study
A **nonfiction** selection tells about things that are real and often has photographs.

K What I Know	W What I Want to Know	L What I Learned

Comprehension Strategy
Monitor Comprehension: Reading Rate Read along smoothly with the rhythm and rhyme of this nonfiction poem. Slow down to read important information.

OKLAHOMA PASS—1RL7.1 know/appreciate various genres; 1RL7.1a discriminate between fiction/nonfiction

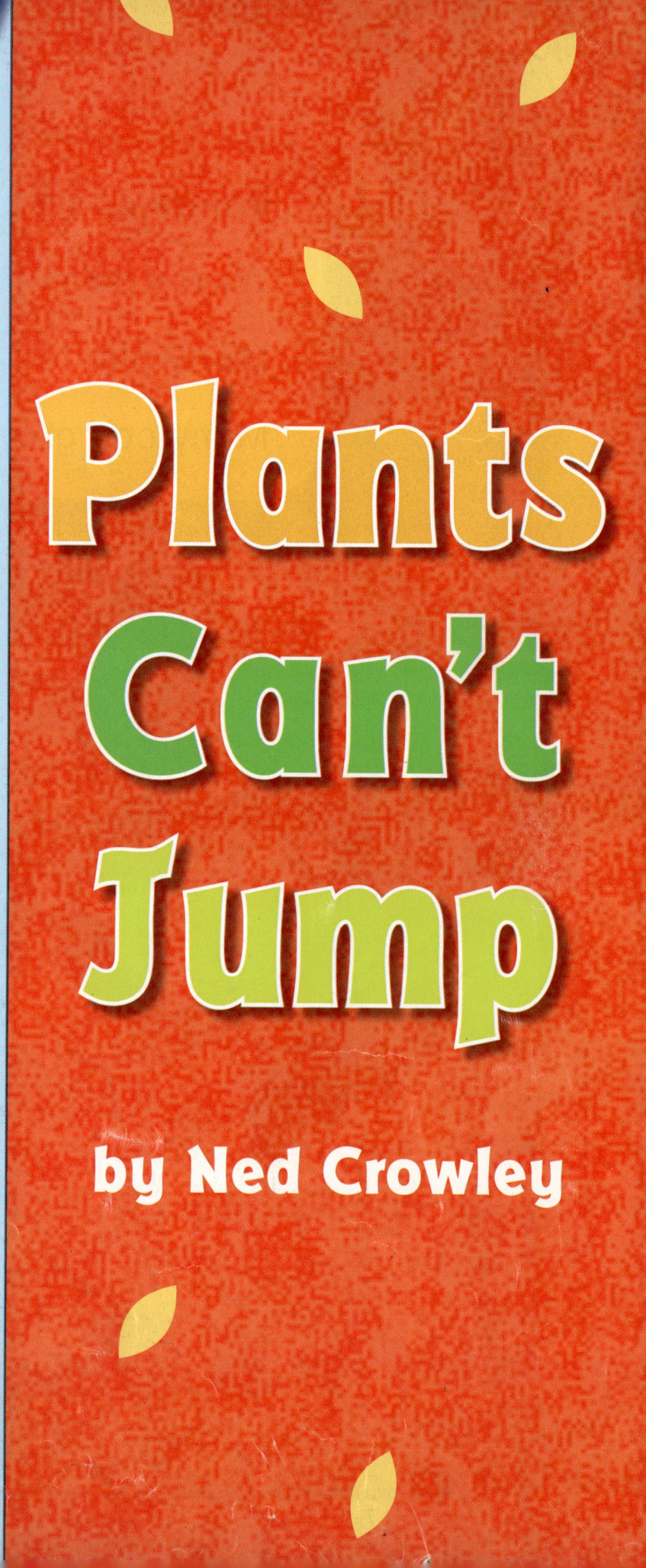

Plants Can't Jump

by Ned Crowley

107

Plants can't jump!
Plants can't hop.

Just add water,
and up they pop!

Roots grow down.
Stems grow up.

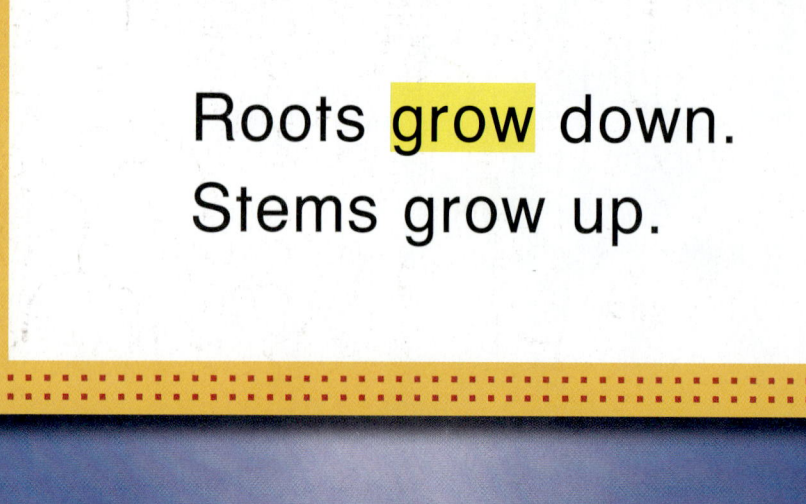

Plants can look like bells and cups.

111

Plants have spots
and dots and bumps.

Plants can be thin.
Plants can be plump.

A plant has leaves,
but what do they give?

Leaves make food so a plant can live.

Plants must get water.
It helps them grow.

Plip, plop, plip!
Where does it go?

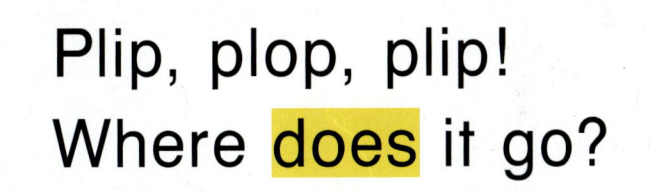

Plants live in sand.
Plants live in mud.

This plant has flowers.
That one has a bud.

If some bugs want food,
they eat plants.

Some plants eat bugs
like moths and ants!

Plants are red
and pink and black.

Many plants are food, so grab a snack!

Plants can't jump,
but they don't fuss.

Plants can grow, just like us!

Think Critically

1. What do leaves do for plants?
   DRAW CONCLUSIONS

2. What do a plant's roots do? What does the stem do? **DETAILS**

3. What are different ways a plant can get water? **DRAW CONCLUSIONS**

4. Why do you think some plants eat bugs? **MAKE INFERENCES**

5. **WRITE** Which do you like better—a plant with flowers or a plant you can eat? Tell why. **WRITING RESPONSE**

OKLAHOMA PASS—1RL4.1 increase vocabulary by listening to/reading a variety of literature; 1RL6.1 demonstrate literal understanding of text; 1RL6.2 make inferences; 1RL8.1d access information from charts/maps/graphs/calendars; 1WG2 use a variety of modes/written forms for various purposes; 1VL1.2 respond to stories/poems through talk/movement/music/art/drama/ writing

Meet the Author
Ned Crowley

Ned Crowley is a writer and illustrator. Recently, he has been writing books about bugs and plants. Mr. Crowley says books like these are fun to write. When he looks at pictures of plants or bugs, he tries to give them personalities just like people.

Mr. Crowley has three daughters. He says that they like plants a lot more than bugs!

www.harcourtschool.com/storytown

Science

Cornfield Leaves
by Lessie Jones Little
illustrated by Don Tate

Poetry

Teacher Read-Aloud

Cornfield Leaves

by Lessie Jones Little
illustrated by Don Tate

Silky ribbons long and green,
Dotted with sparkling dew,
Waving in the summer breeze
Under a roof of blue.

Keep on waving in the breeze,
Keep on sparkling, too,
And every time you wave at me,
I'll wave right back at you

Teacher Read-Aloud

Connections

Comparing Texts   1RL6.1c 1RL6.3b 1RL6.2 1RL7.1

1. How are "Plants Can't Jump" and the poem "Cornfield Leaves" alike?

2. Tell about an interesting plant you have seen at home or at school.

3. What is your favorite food that comes from a plant?

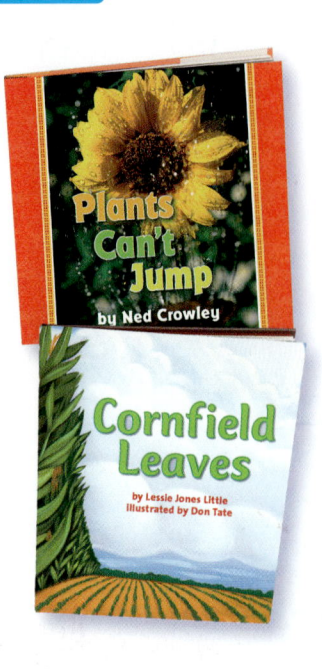

Writing   1RL4.4 1WG2.5 1VL1.2

Draw a picture of your favorite plant. Label the parts of your plant. Write about why you like it.

flower
stem
leaves
roots

I like sunflowers because they grow tall!

130

Phonics 1RL3.1 1RL3.1a

Make and read new words.

Start with **us**.

Add **b** at the beginning.

Change **s** to **d**.

Change **b** to **m**.

Change **d** to **s t**.

Fluency Practice 1RL5.2 1RL5.3 1RL5.4

Read "Plants Can't Jump" to a partner. Pause at the end of each line. Then have your partner read it to you. Tell which part is your favorite.

Plants can't jump! Plants can't hop.

Just add water, and up they pop!

Contents

Get Started Story

"Frog Gets His Song" 134
by Linda Barr • illustrated by Jui Ishida

Read this Get Started Story.

Plot 142
Learn to think about the events that happen in a story.

Words to Know 144
Learn to read and write new high-frequency words.

"Soccer Song" 146
by Patricia Reilly Giff • illustrated by Blanche Sims

- Learn the features of realistic fiction.
- Learn how to recognize the structure of a story.

"Now You Know About Soccer" 164
Learn about playing soccer.

Connections 166
- Compare texts.
- Write about a game or sport I learned to play.
- Practice building words.
- Reread for fluency.

Lesson 10

1 Get Started Story
Frog Gets His Song
by Linda Barr
illustrated by Jui Ishida

2 Genre: Realistic Fiction
Soccer Song
by Patricia Reilly Giff
illustrated by Blanche Sims

3 *Now You Know About Soccer*
Genre: Nonfiction

133

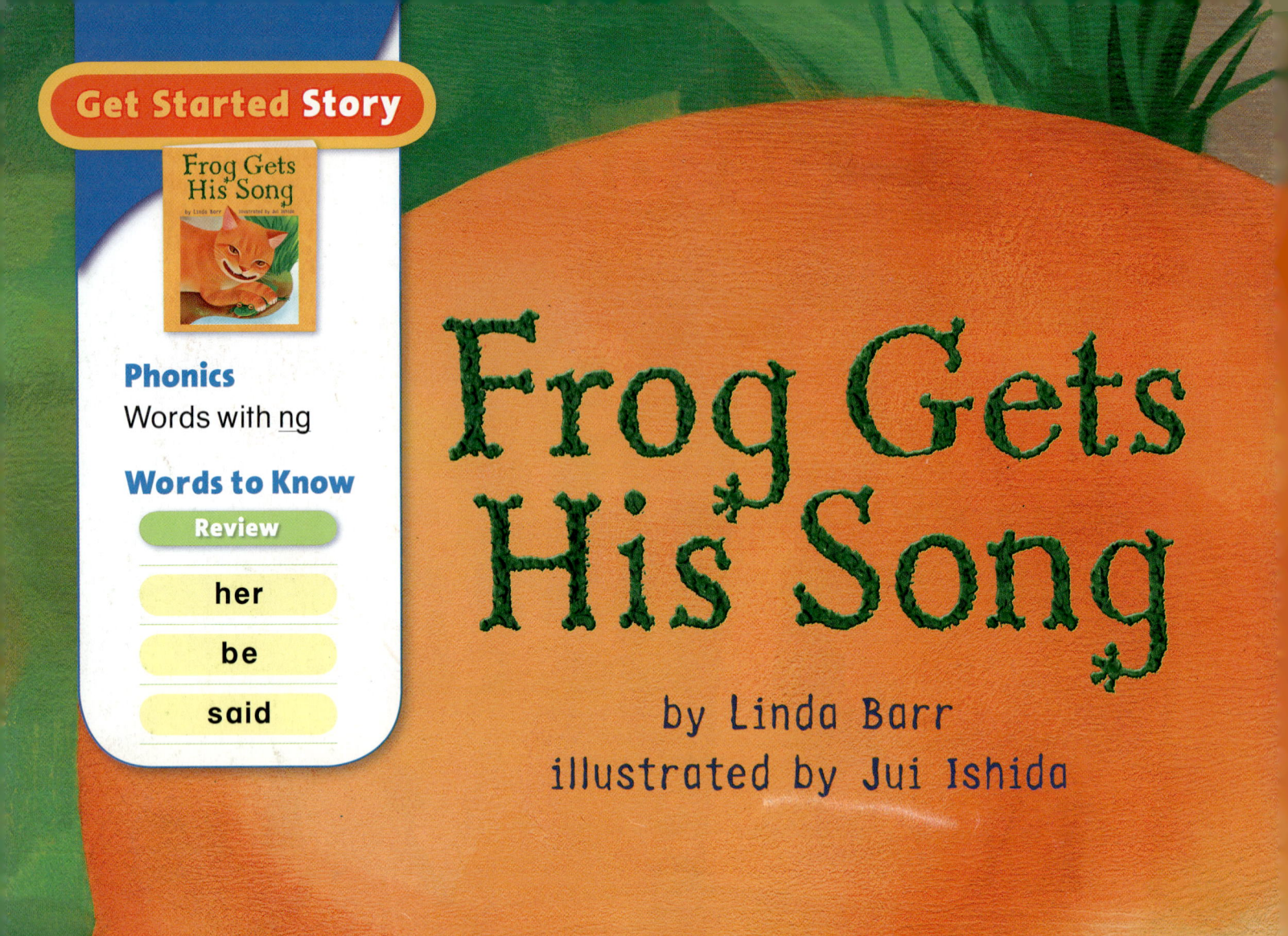

Get Started Story

Phonics
Words with ng

Words to Know
Review
her
be
said

Frog Gets His Song

by Linda Barr
illustrated by Jui Ishida

Ming had Frog in her grip.
Ming looked at him with a big grin.

Frog looked at Ming's long fangs. "Help!" yelled Frog. "Let me go!"

"Be still!" Ming hissed. "Sing me a song and I will let you go."

"Sing?" grunted Frog. "Frogs can't sing!"

"Do frogs have lungs?" Ming asked.

"Yes," Frog said.

"Then sing!" Ming snapped.

Frog filled his lungs and sang. His song rang out. Frog sang and sang and sang.

Did Ming let Frog go? Yes.
Did Frog stop singing? No!

Frogs are still singing!

Focus Skill

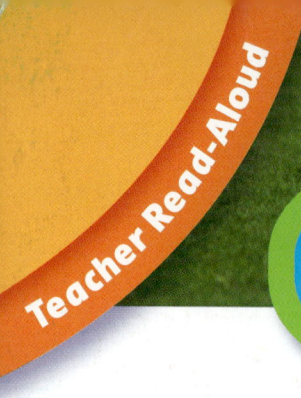

Plot

The events that make up a story are called the **plot**. The **plot** of a story is what happens in that story.

Look at the pictures.

These pictures show a story. The plot is about children finding a lost dog.

The pictures show events in a story.
What is the plot?

Try This!

Look at the picture. Choose the words that name the plot of a story about these people.

- enjoying winter activities
- playing with pets
- having a picnic

www.harcourtschool.com/storytown

OKLAHOMA PASS—1RL7.2b identify/describe plot/setting/characters

Words to Know

High-Frequency Words

- school
- every
- your
- feet
- use
- arms
- head
- way

You can have fun at **school every** day.

Run and jump with **your feet**.

Use your feet to kick the ball.

Use your **arms** and **head**, too.

You can block the ball this **way**.

www.harcourtschool.com/storytown

Soccer Song
Realistic Fiction

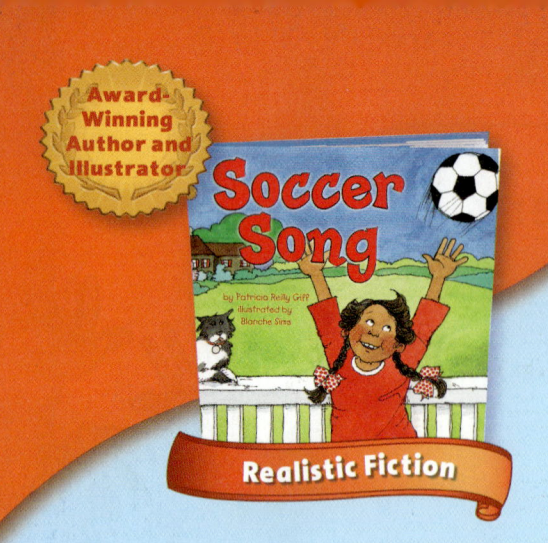

1RL7.1
1RL7.1a

Genre Study
Realistic fiction stories have a beginning, middle, and ending. Characters do things that could happen in real life.

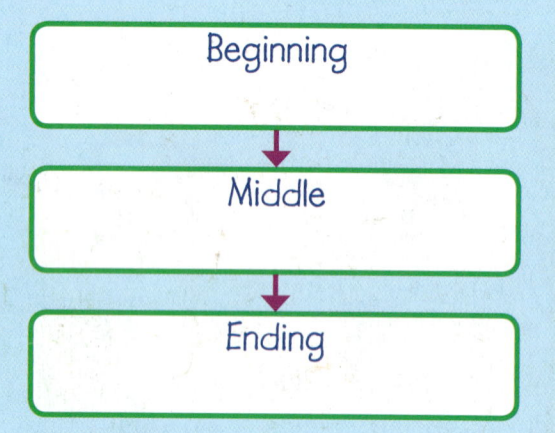

Beginning
↓
Middle
↓
Ending

Comprehension Strategy
Recognize Story Structure As you read, think about what is happening in each part of the story.

OKLAHOMA PASS—1RL7.1 know/appreciate various genres; 1RL7.1a discriminate between fiction/nonfiction.

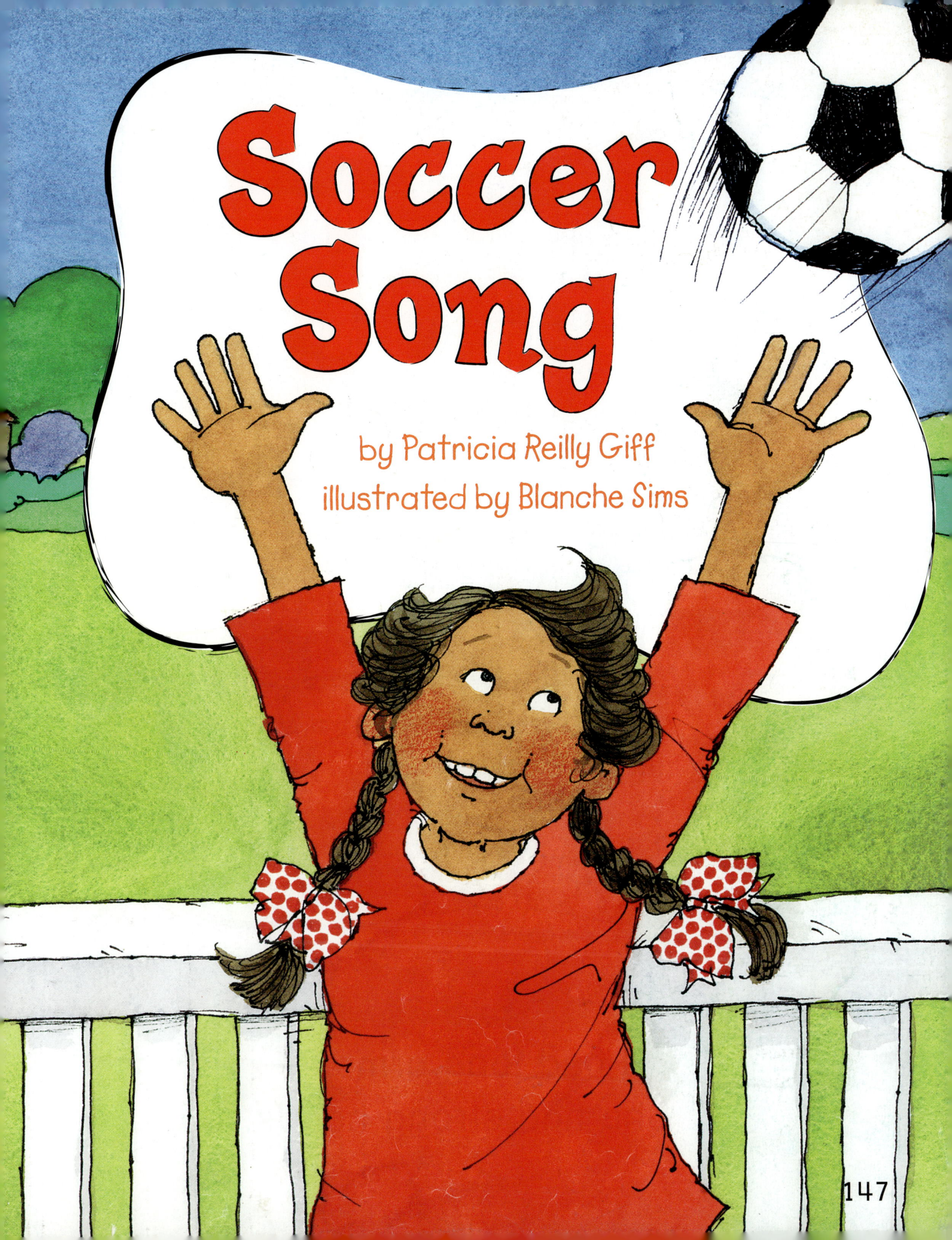

Soccer Song

by Patricia Reilly Giff

illustrated by Blanche Sims

Jill had long arms.
She had strong hands.

One day, Jill got Gus.
"Jill did it!" called Tom.
"Meow," said Gus.

One day, Fran swung the bat.
Her ball went up.
Jill jumped up.

"Jill got it!" yelled the kids.
"Meow," said Gus.

At school, Miss King said, "It's soccer time! Kick the ball with your feet."

"Don't use your hands!" said Tom.

Jill's legs went this way.
The ball went that way.

Jill's head went this way.
The ball went that way.

155

Jill hung her head.

"You have strong arms and hands," said Tom. "You got Gus out of a tree."

"You got my ball, too," said Fran.

"A goalie can use her hands," said Miss King.

The next day, Jill was goalie. She used her strong arms and hands. She blocked the ball every time.

"You did it!" yelled Tom and Fran.

"Jump, block! I am strong!
This is my soccer song!" sang Jill.
"Meow!" sang Gus.

Think Critically

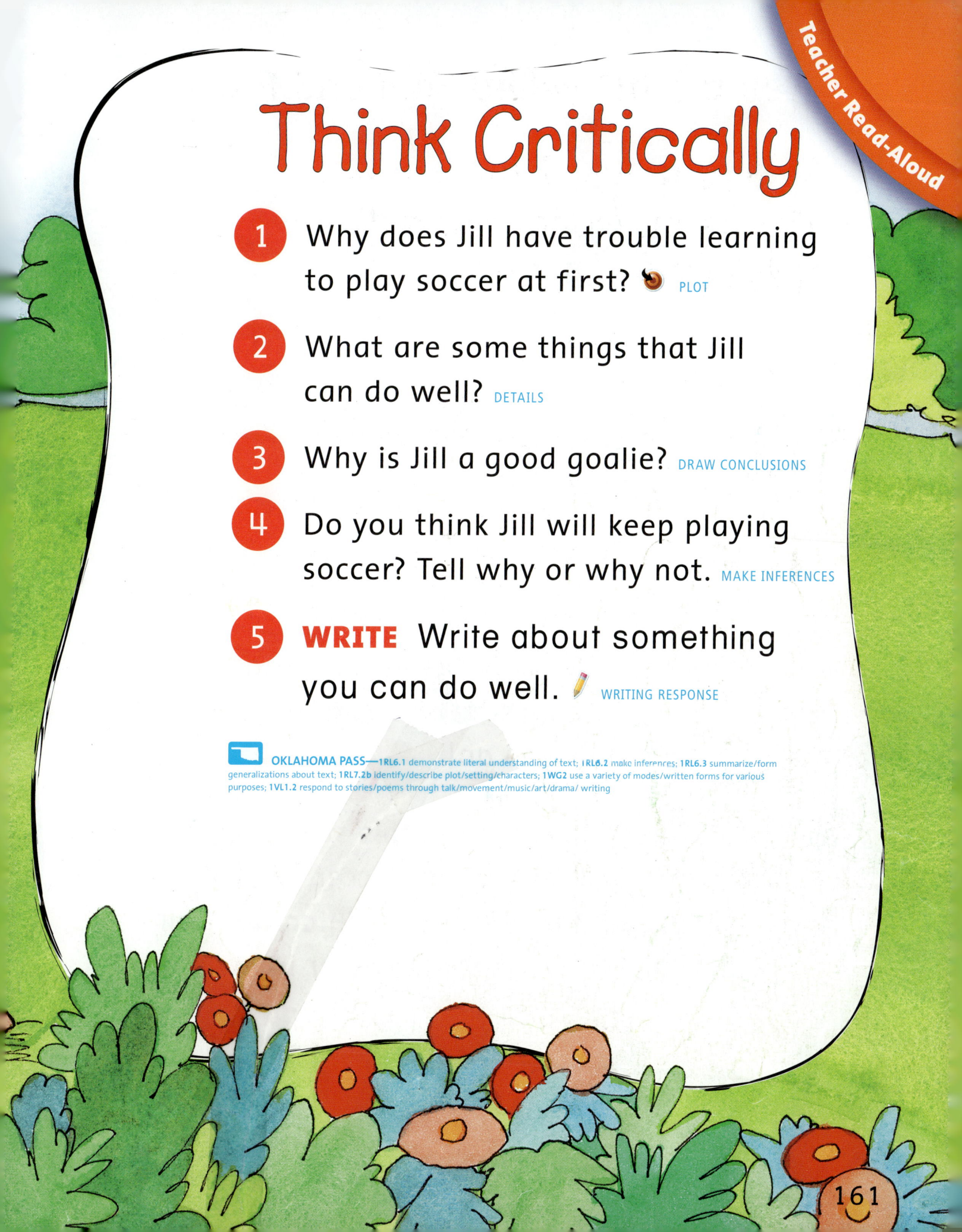

1 Why does Jill have trouble learning to play soccer at first? PLOT

2 What are some things that Jill can do well? DETAILS

3 Why is Jill a good goalie? DRAW CONCLUSIONS

4 Do you think Jill will keep playing soccer? Tell why or why not. MAKE INFERENCES

5 **WRITE** Write about something you can do well. WRITING RESPONSE

OKLAHOMA PASS—1RL6.1 demonstrate literal understanding of text; 1RL6.2 make inferences; 1RL6.3 summarize/form generalizations about text; 1RL7.2b identify/describe plot/setting/characters; 1WG2 use a variety of modes/written forms for various purposes; 1VL1.2 respond to stories/poems through talk/movement/music/art/drama/ writing

Meet the Author
Patricia Reilly Giff

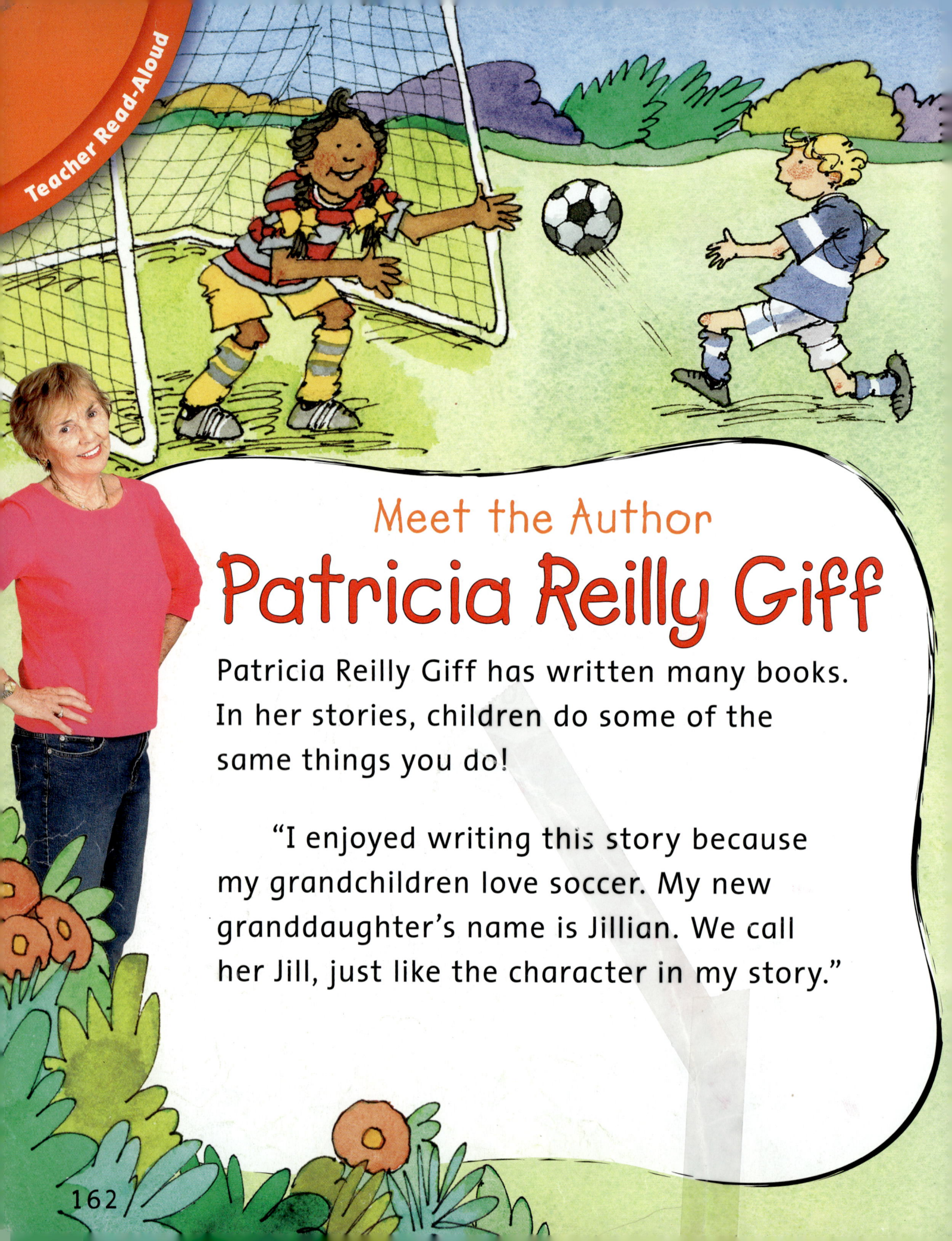

Patricia Reilly Giff has written many books. In her stories, children do some of the same things you do!

"I enjoyed writing this story because my grandchildren love soccer. My new granddaughter's name is Jillian. We call her Jill, just like the character in my story."

Meet the Illustrator
Blanche Sims

Blanche Sims has illustrated many children's books. She says that the best part about being an artist is drawing. She has always loved to draw! When Blanche Sims was in school, one of her teachers even hung up a huge piece of paper in the classroom for her to fill with her artwork.

Meow

www.harcourtschool.com/storytown

Social Studies

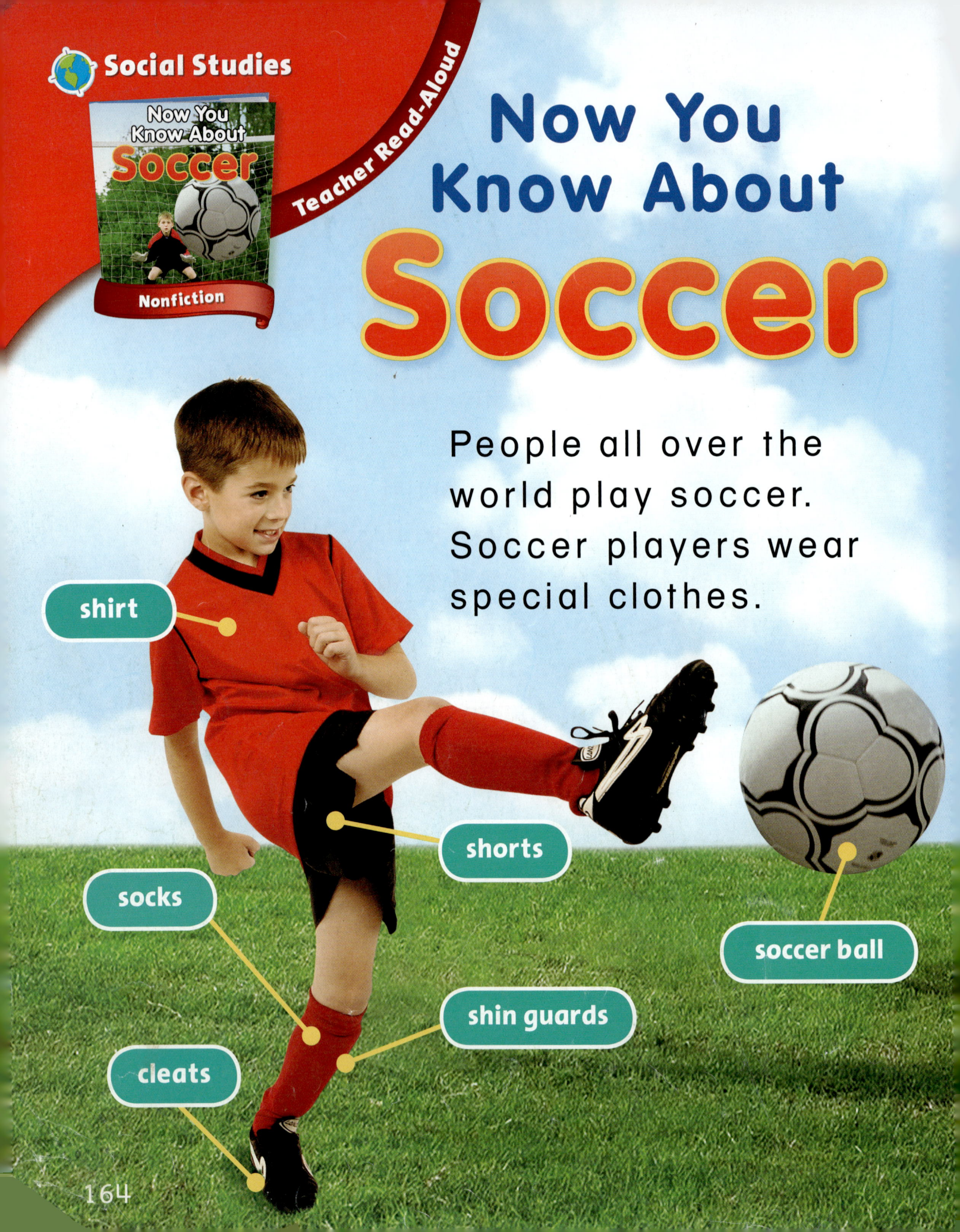

Teacher Read-Aloud

Nonfiction

Now You Know About Soccer

People all over the world play soccer. Soccer players wear special clothes.

- shirt
- shorts
- socks
- soccer ball
- shin guards
- cleats

Teams must practice. It's fun!

A team gets the ball in the other team's goal. One point!

Teams show they are good sports. "Good game!" they say.

Connections

Comparing Texts

1RL6.1c
1RL6.2
1RL7.1

❶ What did you learn about soccer from the story? What more did you learn from the article?

❷ What games and sports have you played at school or at home?

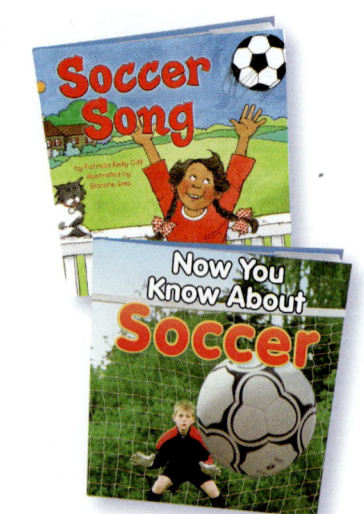

❸ What is your favorite game or sport? Why?

Writing

1WG2.5

Draw a picture of yourself learning to play a game or sport. Write what happened. Write some of the words you said.

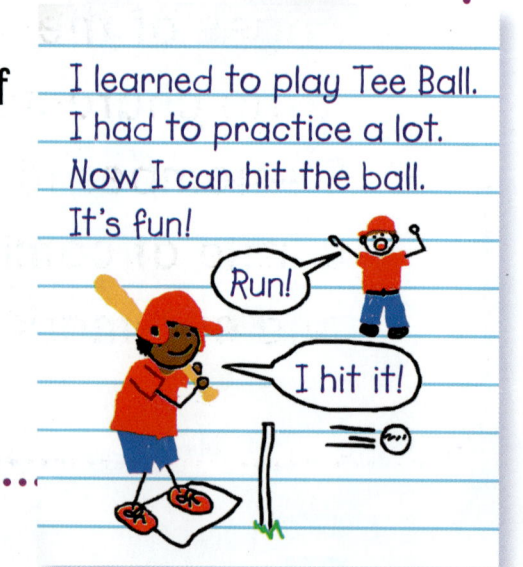

I learned to play Tee Ball.
I had to practice a lot.
Now I can hit the ball.
It's fun!

Run!
I hit it!

Phonics

Make and read new words.

Start with **long**.

Change [l] to [s].

Add [t] [r] after [s].

Change [o] to [i].

Take out [r].

Fluency Practice

Read with a partner. Take turns reading pages of the story. Make it sound as if the characters are really talking. Remember to pause a little at commas and end marks.

Contents

Get Started Story

"Sid Scores" 170
by Deanne W. Kells • illustrated by Pierre Pratt
Read this Get Started Story.

Words with or and ore 178
Practice reading words with or and ore.

Words to Know 180
Learn to read and write new high-frequency words.

"Land of Ice" 182
by Norbert Wu
- Learn the features of nonfiction.
- Learn to make inferences.

"My Father's Feet" 204
Listen to a poem about penguins by Judy Sierra.

Connections 206
- Compare texts.
- Write sentences to tell about the land of ice.
- Practice building words.
- Reread for fluency.

Lesson 11

1 Get Started Story

Sid Scores
by Deanne W. Kells illustrated by Pierre Pratt

2 Genre: Nonfiction

Land of Ice
by Norbert Wu

3

My Father's Feet
by Judy Sierra

Genre: Poetry

Get Started Story

Phonics
Words with or

Words to Know
Review

lives
was
now

Sid Scores

by Deanne W. Kells
illustrated by Pierre Pratt

170

Sid lives in the North.
He likes all sports.

Sid was born to win.
Sid scores and scores.
Win, Sid, win!

Sid can swim more than six laps.
He has good form.

Sid can do more.
He can jump past the cord.

Sid can flip and flop.
He can skim and skid.
More, Sid, more!

Sid is sore and worn out.
He will rest now.

Sid will snort and snore.
Sid will score more in the morning.

Phonics Skill

Words with or and ore

The letters **or** and **ore** can stand for the sound at the beginning of **orange**, in the middle of **fork**, and at the end of **store**.

orange

fork

store

Look at each picture. Read the words. Which word tells about the picture?

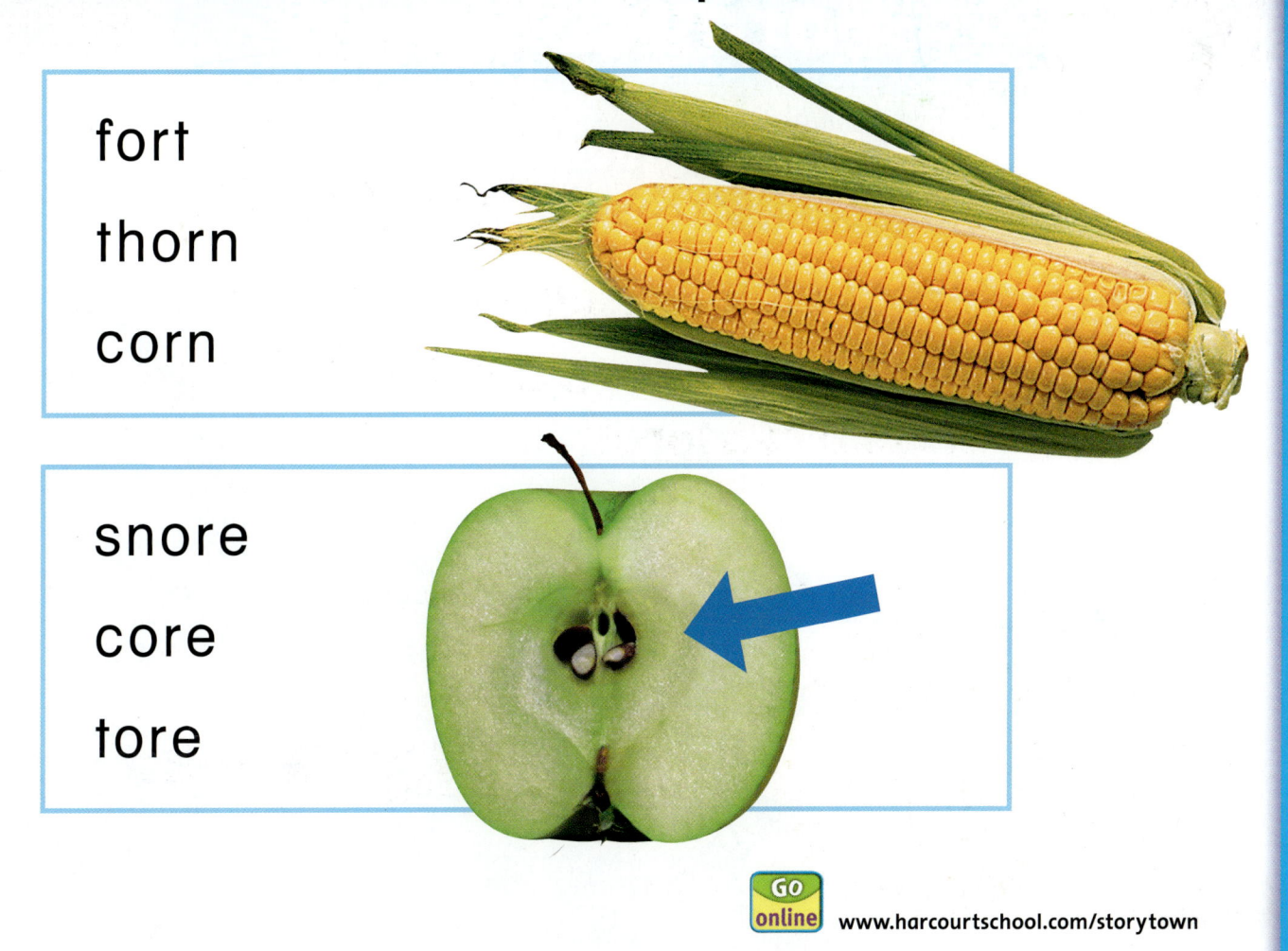

fort

thorn

corn

snore

core

tore

www.harcourtschool.com/storytown

Try This!

Read the sentences.

We went to the store for food. My mom got some corn. My dad got more eggs. I got a new hat and wore it home.

OKLAHOMA PASS—1RL3.1 decode one-syllable words; 1RL3.1b decode using r-controlled vowel patterns

Words to Know

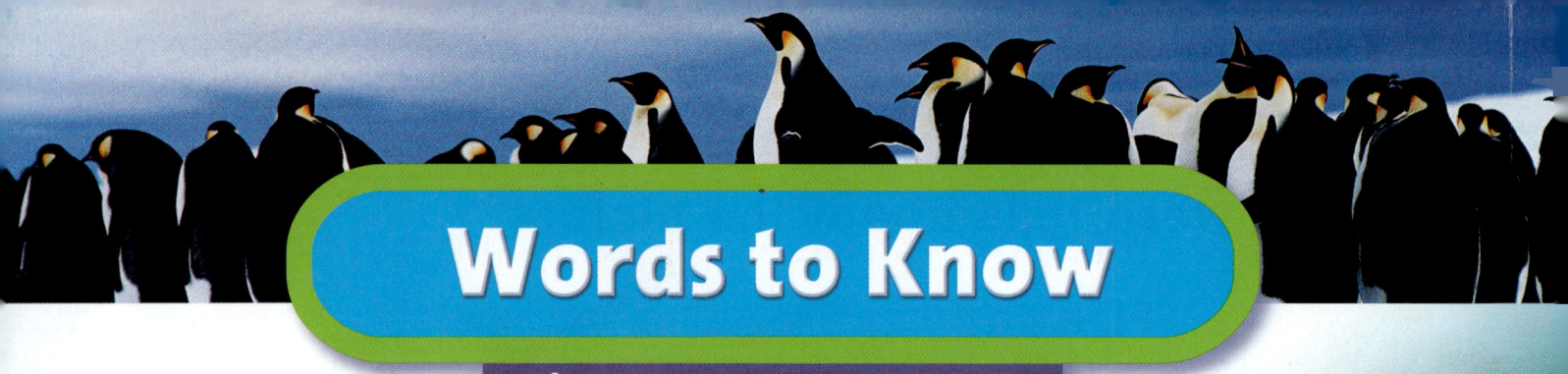

High-Frequency Words

- very
- cold
- fish
- their
- from
- animals
- under

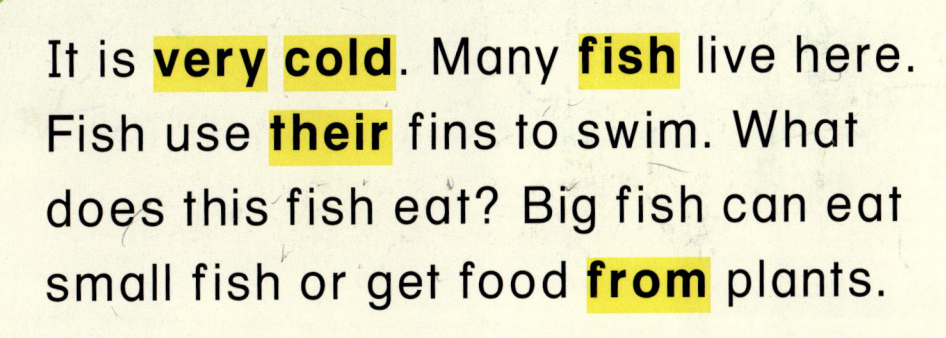

It is **very cold**. Many **fish** live here. Fish use **their** fins to swim. What does this fish eat? Big fish can eat small fish or get food **from** plants.

More **animals** live here. Many of them can swim **under** the water, too.

www.harcourtschool.com/storytown

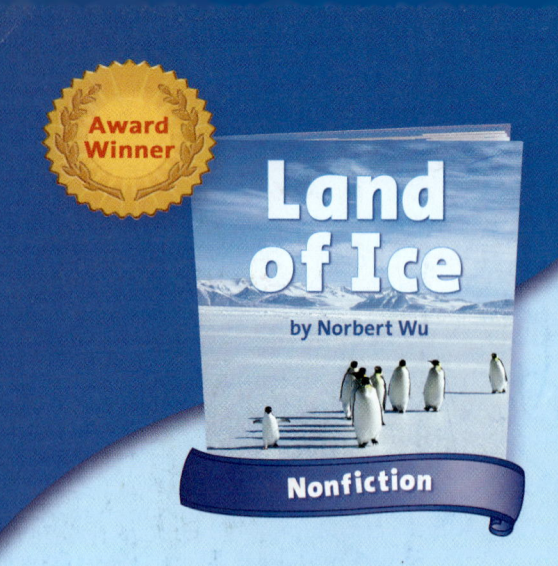

Award Winner

Land of Ice
by Norbert Wu

Nonfiction

1RL7.1
1RL7.1a
Genre Study
A **nonfiction** selection gives many facts about real things and often has photographs.

Comprehension Strategy
1RL6.2
Monitor Comprehension: Make Inferences Think about what the words say and what you already know to figure out what the selection is about.

OKLAHOMA PASS—1RL6.2 make inferences; 1RL7.1 know/appreciate various genres; 1RL7.1a discriminate between fiction/nonfiction

182

Land of Ice

by Norbert Wu

This is a land of ice.
It is very cold.

What is out here?
Can things live in
this land?

185

Look! This is a seal with a small pup that was just born. How can seals live here?

Seals have lots of fat and thick fur. This makes them snug.

Here is a small penguin.

This sort of penguin makes nests on rocks and cliffs. Penguins come from eggs.

Do more things live here?
Let's go under the ice.

It's beautiful! You can still see the sun.

You can see red sea stars.

There are animals that look like plants!

193

You can see an octopus, too.

This animal has long strings that sting small animals. This helps it get its food.

This small fish likes ice. It does not get too cold. It has a nest of eggs in the ice.

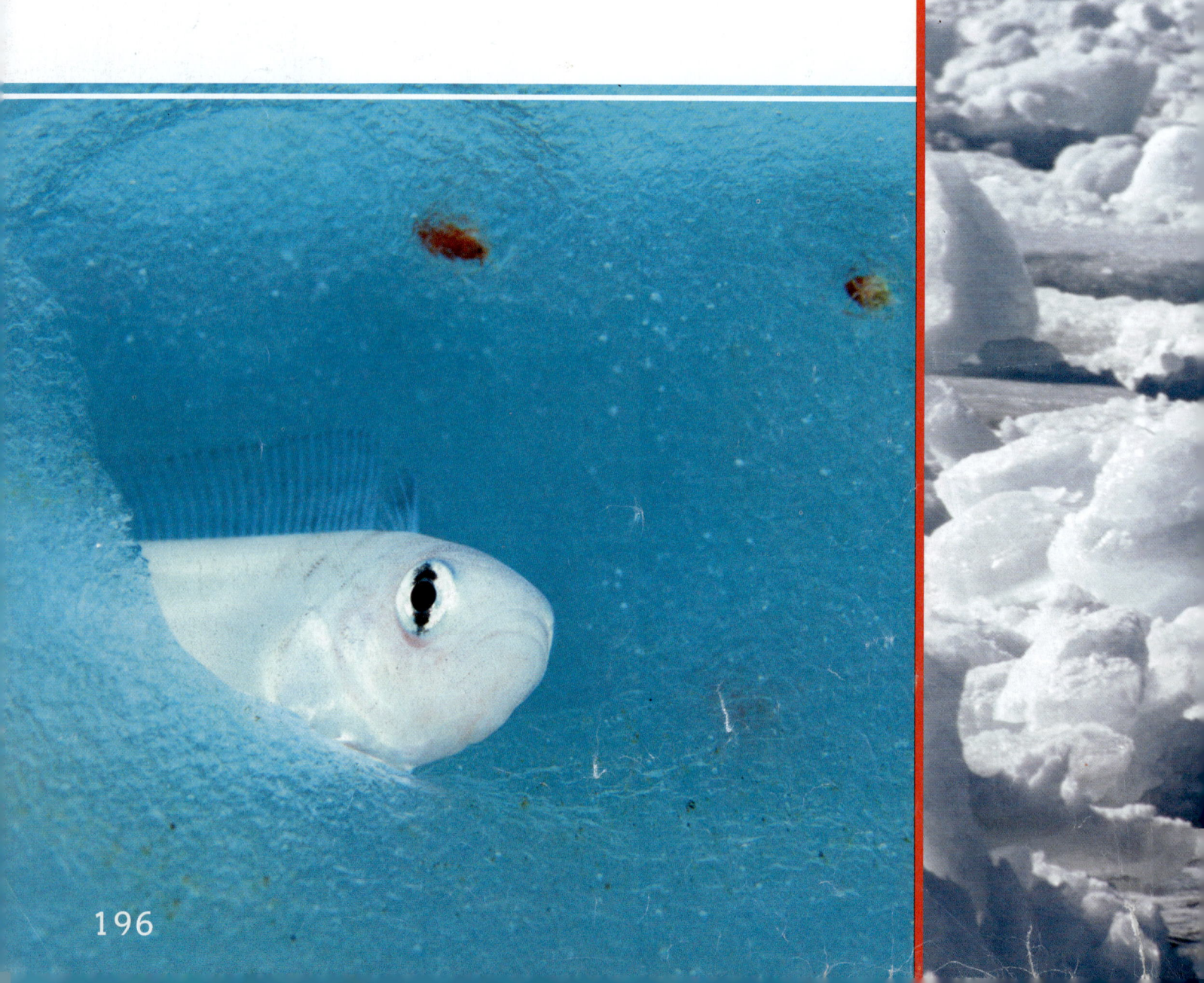

This mom is helping her little one swim in the cold water.

Here are some more penguins.
Look at them go!

They use their wings to swim very fast. Flap, flap, flap! Where will they go next?

199

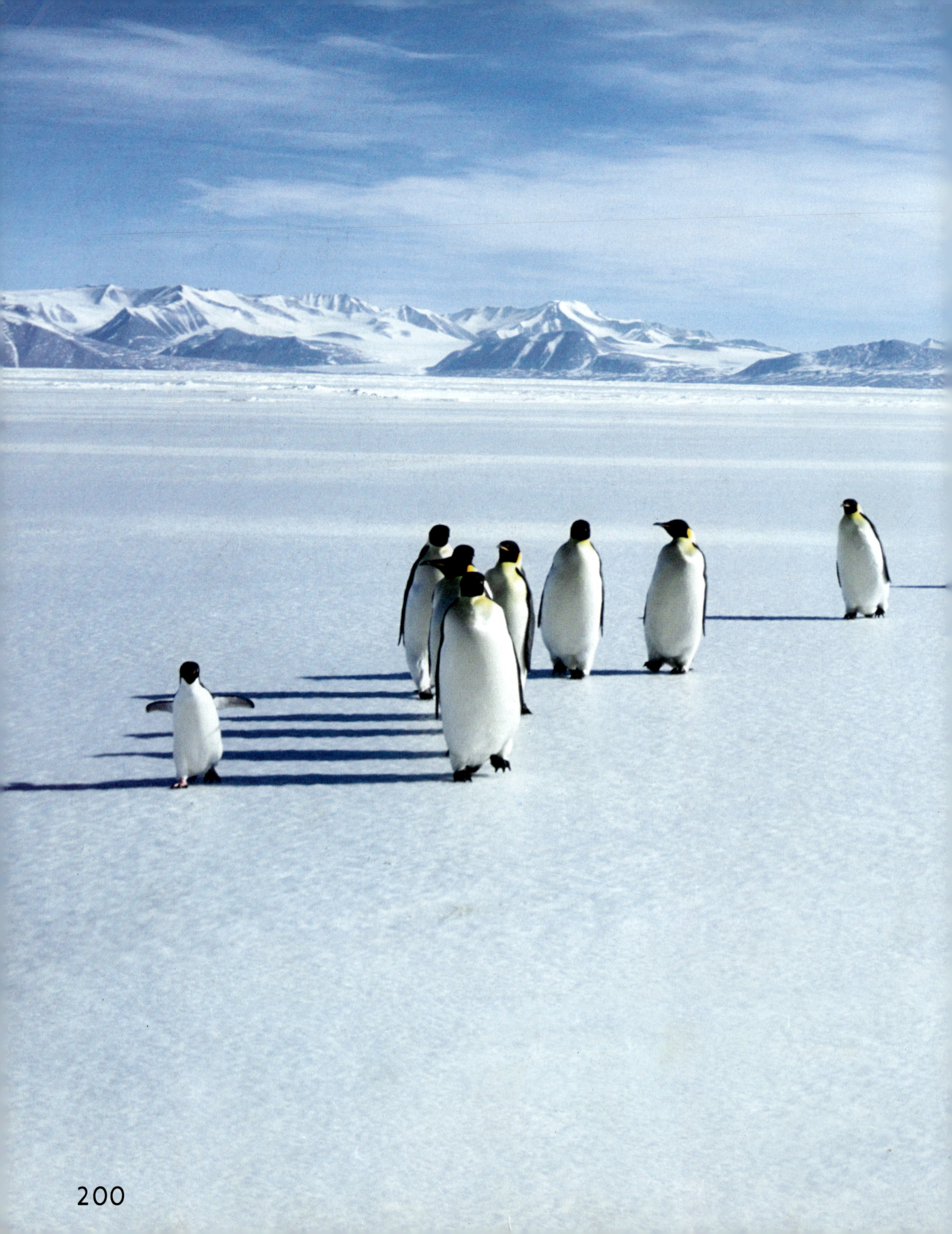

This IS a land of ice...
and much more!

Teacher Read-Aloud

Think Critically

1. How is the land different from what is under the water? How is it the same? **COMPARE AND CONTRAST**

2. What are some animals that live in the land of ice? **DETAILS**

3. Why do you think penguins like to live there? **DRAW CONCLUSIONS**

4. Does it look as if people could live there? Why or why not? **MAKE INFERENCES**

5. **WRITE** Write about the most interesting animal in "Land of Ice."
   WRITING RESPONSE

OKLAHOMA PASS—1RL6.1 demonstrate literal understanding of text; 1RL6.2 make inferences; 1RL6.4 analyze/evaluate text; 1RL7.2b identify/describe plot/setting/characters; 1WG2.5 write brief descriptions using details; 1VL1.2 respond to stories/poems through talk/movement/music/art/drama/writing

Meet the Author/Photographer
Norbert Wu

Norbert Wu likes to take pictures in unusual places, like under the ice in Antarctica! He has seen many animals there, including lots of penguins. He says that penguins walk oddly on land, but are at home in the water. They swim around fast, just like little jet planes!

"I wrote this story because I want you to know that our world is a beautiful and fragile place."

www.harcourtschool.com/storytown

Science

My Father's Feet
by Judy Sierra
Poetry

Teacher Read-Aloud

My Father's Feet

by Judy Sierra

To keep myself up off the ice,
I find my father's feet are nice.
I snuggle in his belly fluff,
And that's how I stay warm enough.

But when my father takes a walk,
My cozy world begins to rock.
He shuffles left, I hold on tight.
Oh no! He's wobbling to the right.

Not left again! Oops, here he goes.
Do you suppose my father knows
I'm hanging on to his warm toes?

Teacher Read-Aloud

Connections

Comparing Texts 1RL6.2 1RL6.4

1. Would the penguins from the poem like the land of ice? Tell why or why not.

2. How is the place in "Land of Ice" like where you live? How is it different?

3. What would you do in the land of ice?

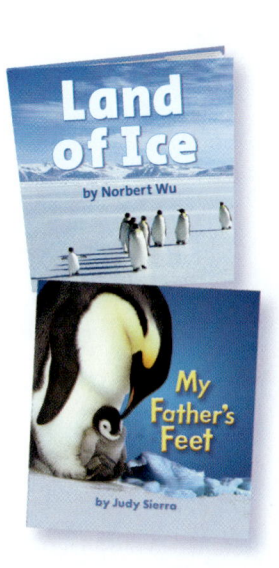

Writing 1WG2.5

Write sentences about "Land of Ice." Tell what you would see, hear, smell, taste, and feel if you were there.

The land of ice is very cold. There is snow and ice all around.

Phonics

1RL3.1
1RL3.1b

Make and read new words.

Start with **for**.

Add [t] at the end.

Change [f] to [s].

Change [t] to [e].

Change [s] to [m].

Fluency Practice

1RL5.3
1RL5.4
1RL5.5

Read a favorite part of the story or poem to a partner. Stop a little at end marks and commas to help you read one "chunk" at a time.

OKLAHOMA PASS—1RL3.1 decode one-syllable words; 1RL3.1b decode using r-controlled vowel patterns; 1RL5.3 engage in repeated readings to increase fluency; 1RL5.4 recognize high-frequency/common irregularly spelled words; 1RL5.5 use punctuation cues to understand meaning; 1RL6.2 make inferences; 1RL6.4 analyze/evaluate text; 1WG2.5 write brief descriptions using details

Contents

Get Started Story

"Fox and His Big Wish" 210
by Sandra Widener • illustrated by Will Terry

Read this Get Started Story.

Setting 218

Learn to identify when and where a story takes place.

Words to Know 220

Learn to read and write new high-frequency words.

"King Midas and His Gold" 222
by Patricia and Fredrick McKissack • illustrated by Josée Masse

- Learn the features of a myth.
- Learn to ask myself questions while I read.

"Gold and Money" 244

Learn about a golden coin and how different states have special coins.

Connections 246

- Compare texts.
- Write lists.
- Practice building words.
- Reread for fluency.

Lesson 12

1 Get Started Story

Fox and His Big Wish
by Sandra Widener
Illustrated by Will Terry

2 Genre: Myth

King Midas and His Gold
by Patricia and Fredrick McKissack
Illustrated by Josée Masse

3 Genre: Nonfiction

Gold and Money

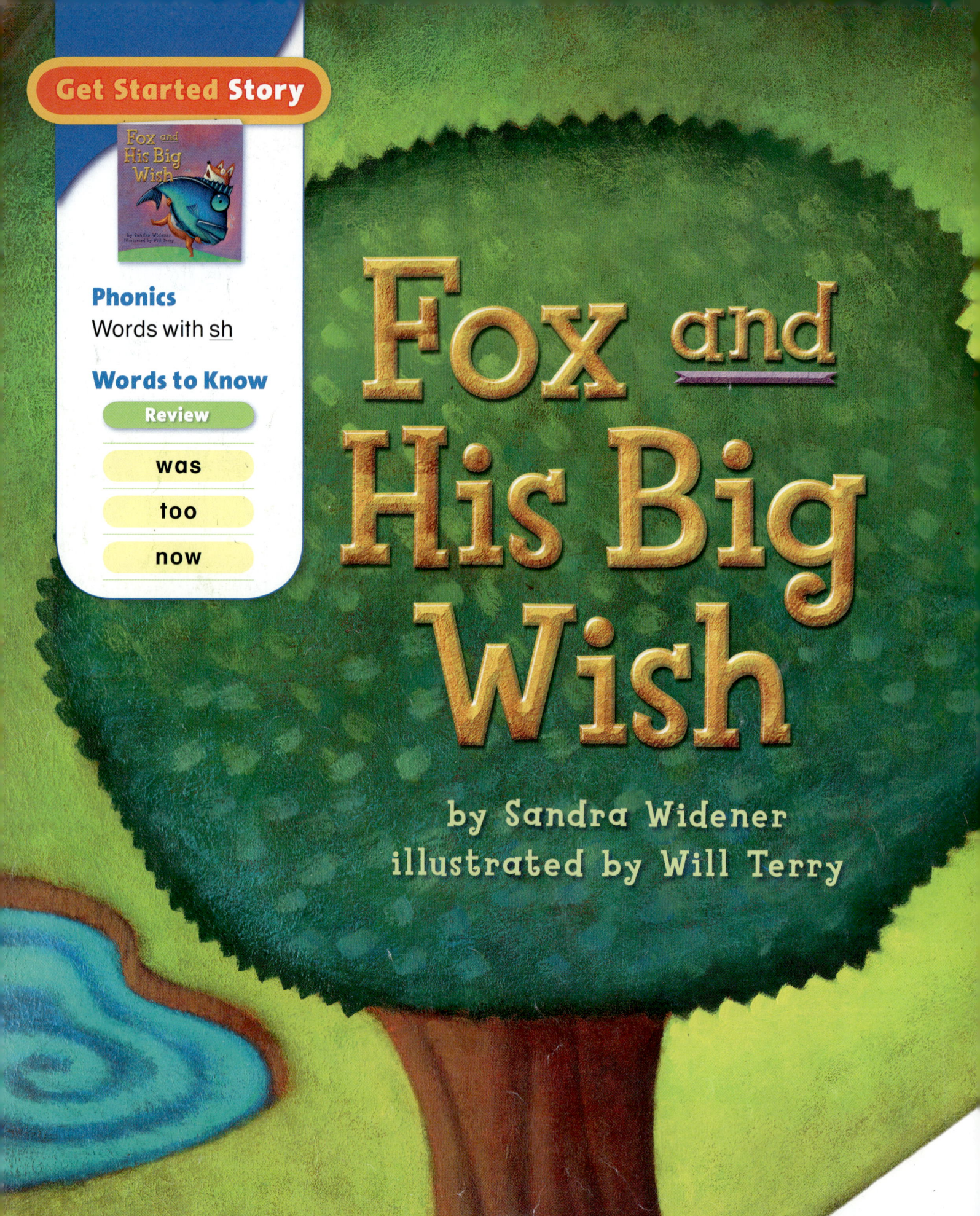

Get Started Story

Phonics
Words with sh

Words to Know
Review
was
too
now

Fox and His Big Wish

by Sandra Widener
illustrated by Will Terry

Fox wanted a snack.
He wished for a big, fresh fish.

Ping!
Fox got his wish!

The fish was big.
It was too big for a snack.

Fox's fish was too big for his dish.
It was too big for his mat.

His fish was not a fresh fish now.
It smelled bad!

Fox did not like his big fish.
He wished that fish was small.

Fox did not get his wish.
That fish went in the trash!

Focus Skill

Setting

The **setting** is when and where the story takes place.

Look at the picture.

The setting is a city at night.

Tell about this picture. What is the setting? How can you tell?

Try This!

Look at the picture. Choose the words that name the setting.

- a day at the zoo
- an evening at the beach
- a day at the park

www.harcourtschool.com/storytown

OKLAHOMA PASS—1RL7.2b identify/describe plot/setting/characters

219

Words to Know

High-Frequency Words

- could
- happy
- gold
- night
- saw
- came
- made
- were

The king asked, "What **could** make me **happy**? Will this **gold** apple make me happy?"

That **night**, the king **saw** a dog. The dog **came** up to him. It licked the king's hand. This **made** the king grin. From then on, they **were** very happy!

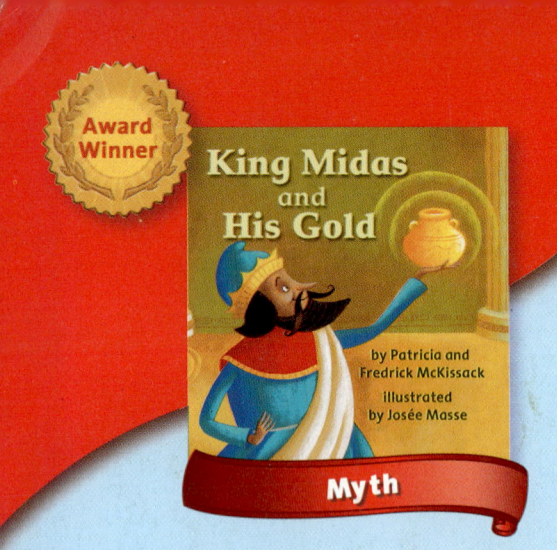

Award Winner

King Midas and His Gold
by Patricia and Fredrick McKissack
illustrated by Josée Masse

Myth

1RL7.1
1RL7.1a
Genre Study
A **myth** is an old story that teaches a lesson. It has make-believe characters and events.

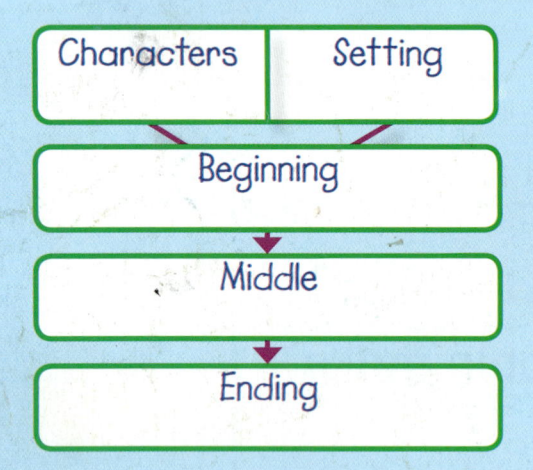

Characters → Setting
↓
Beginning
↓
Middle
↓
Ending

1RL6.5
Comprehension Strategy
Ask Questions As you read, ask yourself questions and look for the answers. Where does King Midas get gold?

OKLAHOMA PASS—1RL6.5 use monitoring/correction strategies (semantics /syntax/ graphophonic cues); 1RL7.1 know/appreciate various genres; 1RL7.1a discriminate between fiction/nonfiction

222

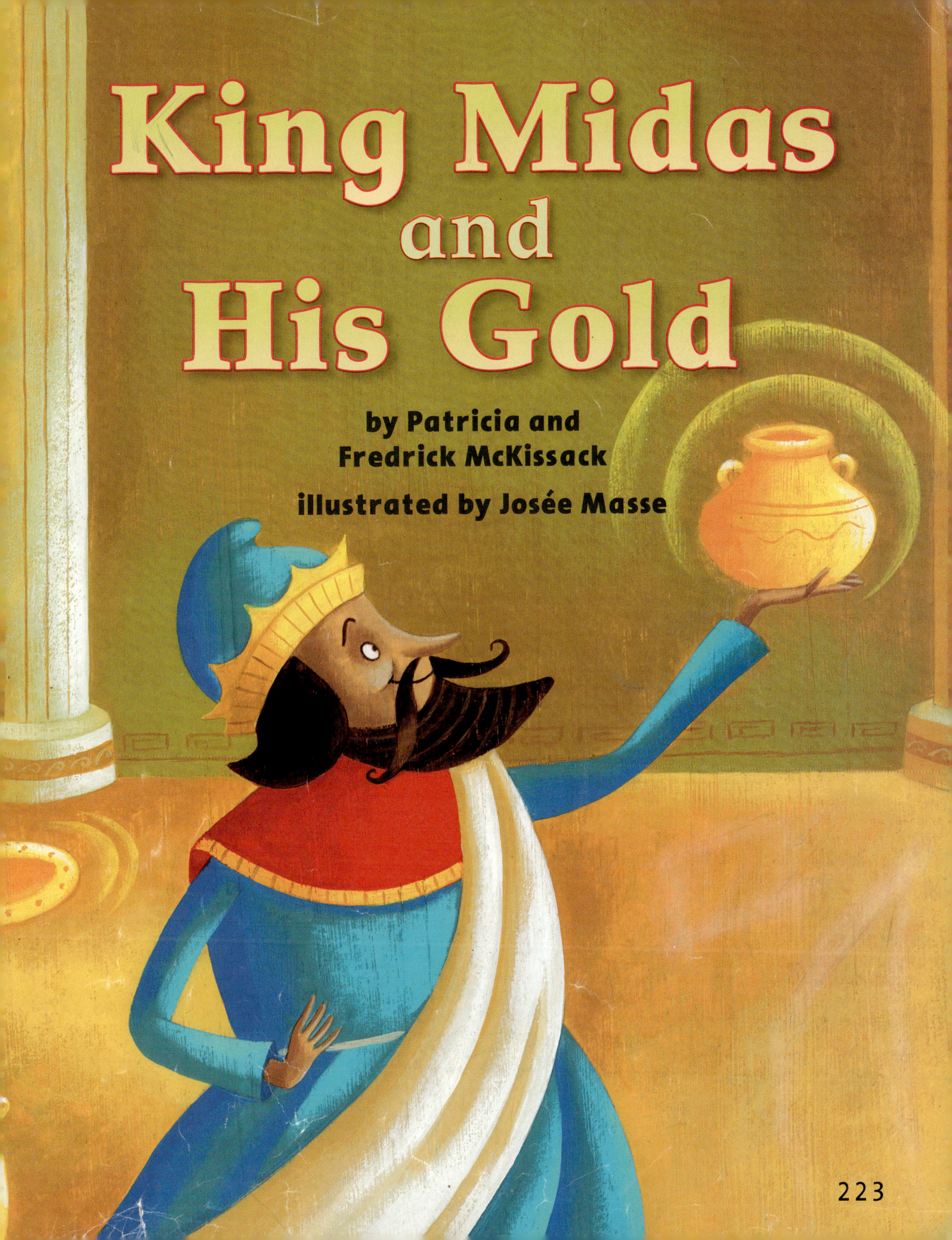

King Midas and His Gold

by Patricia and Fredrick McKissack

illustrated by Josée Masse

Midas was king, but he wasn't happy. "I wish for gold," he said. "That will make me happy."

Ping!
The king got his wish.

King Midas picked a fresh apple.
Ping!
In a flash, it was gold.

Ping! Ping! Ping! Ping!
His cup, dish, box, and shelf
were gold.

King Midas felt happy. He had more and more gold!

King Midas saw a red flower.
Ping! It was gold. King Midas
did not like that.

The king's dog rushed up to him.

Ping! His dog was gold. King Midas did not like that at all.

King Midas was king, but he was not very happy. He **could** not eat a thing.

Ping! Ping!
King Midas could not rest at night.
His blanket and his bed were gold.

233

Ping! His pet cat was gold.
Ping! The queen was gold.

"Get back!" cried the king.
"GET BACK!"

Ping!
The princess was gold.
The king was shocked!

All he had was gold and more gold!
King Midas felt very sad.
"I wish for no more gold," he said.
He got his wish.

Ping!
Back came the princess, the queen, his cat, his dog, the flower, the apple, and all of his things!

King Midas could eat and rest.

"No more gold," he said, and this made him happy.

Think Critically

1. How can you tell that this story takes place long ago? **SETTING**

2. What happens to the apple when the king touches it? **DETAILS**

3. Why doesn't the king like it when his dog turns to gold? **MAKE INFERENCES**

4. Why is King Midas glad to lose his golden touch? **DRAW CONCLUSIONS**

5. **WRITE** Write about something you wish for and tell why. **WRITING RESPONSE**

OKLAHOMA PASS—1RL6.1 demonstrate literal understanding of text; 1RL6.2 make inferences; 1RL7.2b identify/describe plot/setting/characters; 1WG2 use a variety of modes/written forms for various purposes; 1VL1.2 respond to stories/poems through talk/movement/music/art/drama/writing

Teacher Read-Aloud

Meet the Authors

Patricia and Fredrick McKissack

Patricia and Fredrick McKissack met when they were teenagers. Before they began writing books together, Fredrick owned a construction company. Patricia was a teacher. They especially like to write books that show how a person solves a problem.

Meet the Illustrator
Josée Masse

Josée Masse started drawing when she was very young. Her father was a painter. As a child, she would draw with him in his studio.

Josée Masse has pets—a dog, a cat, many fish, and things her daughter brings from outside, like bugs!

www.harcourtschool.com/storytown

Social Studies

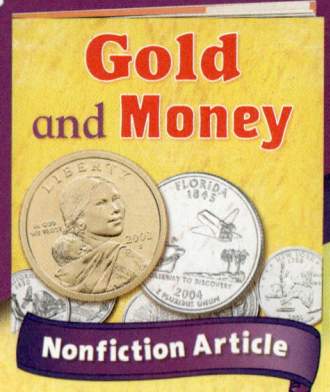

Gold and Money
Nonfiction Article

Teacher Read-Aloud

Gold and Money

The United States has a golden coin. It is worth one dollar.

front back

It shows Sacajawea. Long ago, she helped explorers find their way across America.

244

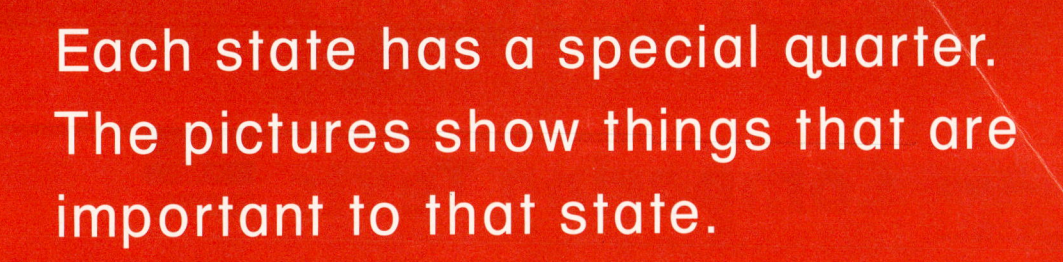

Each state has a special quarter. The pictures show things that are important to that state.

Florida Quarter

front

back

245

Connections

Comparing Texts 1RL6.2 1RL6.3b 1OL2.2

❶ Do you think King Midas would want the coins from "Gold and Money"? Why or why not?

❷ What do you think makes people happy?

❸ Tell about a place that makes you happy. Why are you happy there?

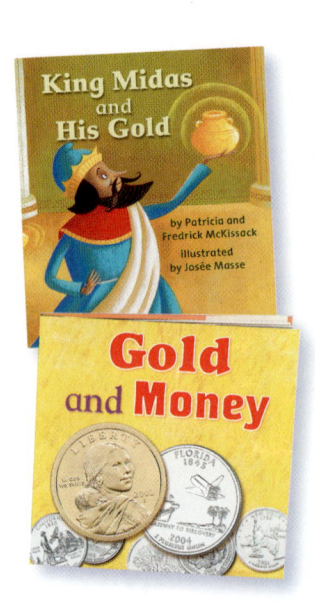

Writing 1WG2

Write Happy on one side of a chart and Sad on the other. List the things that you think make King Midas happy and sad.

Happy	Sad
drink	gold food
rest	gold dog
family	gold bed

246

Phonics

Make and read new words.

Start with **hut**.

Add [s] in front of [h].

Change [s] [h] to [r].

Change [t] to [s] [h].

Change [r] to [w] and [u] to [i].

Fluency Practice

Read the story aloud with classmates. Look for exclamation points. Use your voice to show excitement and other strong feelings.

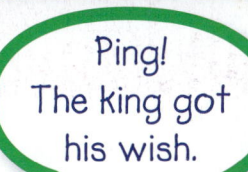

Ping! The king got his wish.

Glossary

What Is a Glossary?

A glossary can help you read a word. You can look up the word and read it in a sentence. Each word has a picture to help you.

gift   Jill got a **gift**.

A

animals — The **animals** have fur.

arms — She is holding out her **arms.**

C

cold My hands are **cold!**

D

day We run all **day.**

E

eat This snack is good to **eat.**

F

feet — Here are my **feet**.

fish — The **fish** is in the water.

food — Look at all the **food**!

G

gold   The girl has **gold**.

grow   I **grow** a little every day.

H

happy   Jack is so **happy!**

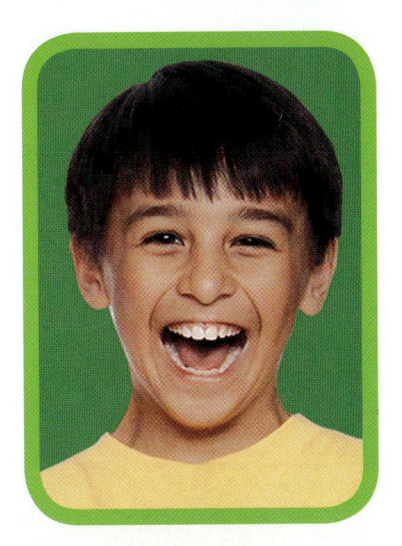

head   I have a hat on my **head.**

L

line   I made a **line** with string.

N

new   She got something **new.**

night   He went to bed last **night.**

S

school   This is my **school**.

T

time   What **time** is it?

U

under   She is **under** it.

W

water   We splash in the **water**.

Acknowledgments
For permission to reprint copyrighted material, grateful acknowledgment is made to the following sources:

Curtis Brown, Ltd.: Adapted from *King Midas and His Gold* by Patricia and Fredrick McKissack. Text copyright © 1986 by Regensteiner Publishing Enterprises, Inc.

Harcourt, Inc.: "My Father's Feet" from *Antarctic Antics: A Book of Penguin Poems* by Judy Sierra. Text copyright © 1998 by Judy Sierra.

Lee & Low Books Inc.: "Cornfield Leaves" from *Children of Long Ago* by Lessie Jones Little. Text copyright © 2000 by Weston W. Little, Sr. Estate; text copyright © 1988 by Weston Little.

Photo Credits
Placement Key: (t) top; (b) bottom; (l) left; (r) right; (c) center; (bg) background; (fg) foreground; (i) inset

5 (t) The Grand Design /SuperStock; 12 (c) The Grand Design / SuperStock; 15 (b) Burke/Triolo Productions/FoodPix/PictureQuest; 24 (bl) Raymond Kasprzak RF/Shutterstock; (cr) Wilmy van Ulft RF/ Shutterstock; 46 (b) Makoto Fujio/Dex Image/PictureQuest; 53 (b) C Squared Studios/Getty Images; 55 Nicholas Piccillo RF/Shutterstock; 88 (bc) Frasnk Cezus/Getty Images; (t) Getty Images; (br) Steve Satushek/ Getty Images; 89 (l) Masterfile Royalty Free; (r) Primsa /Superstock; 93 (bl) Food Collection/Getty Images; 102 Anette Linnea Rasmussen RF/Shutterstock; Jakez RF/Shutterstock; 104 (t) Leonid Nishko RF/ Shutterstock; (b) photocuisine/Corbis; 112 Jim Brandenburg/Minden Pictures; 143 (br) Tom Rosenthal/SuperStock; 164 (br) Wide Group/Getty Images; 165 (tl) (c) Charles Gupton / CORBIS; (cl) Amdrew Olney / Getty Images; (bg) Estelle Klawitter/zefa/ Corbis; (bl) Lynn Siler Photography/ Alamy; 166 (t) Ariel Skelley/Corbis; 169 (b) age fotostock/SuperStock; 178 Silense; RF/Shutterstock; Stanislav Khrapov; RF/Shutterstock; 181 © 2005 Norbert Wu, www.norbertwu.com; 182 (c) Norbert Wu/norbertwu. com; 183 (c) Christian McDonald/www.norbertwu.com; (br) (tr) (cr) (br) Norbert Wu/norbertwu.com; 184-201 Norbert Wu/norbertwu.com; 206 (t) giangrande alessia RF/Shutterstock; 209 (bl) Brand X/SuperStock; 219 Dóri O'Connell RF/Shutterstock; lullabi RF/Shutterstock; Rafa Irusta RF/Shutterstock; 245 United States coin image from the United States Mint.

All other photos © Harcourt School Publishers. Harcourt photos provided by Harcourt Index, Harcourt IPR, and Harcourt Photographers: Weronica Ankarorn, Eric Camden, Doug DuKane, Ken Kinsie, April Riehm and Steve Williams.

Illustration Credits
Cover Art; Laura and Eric Ovresat, Artlab, Inc.

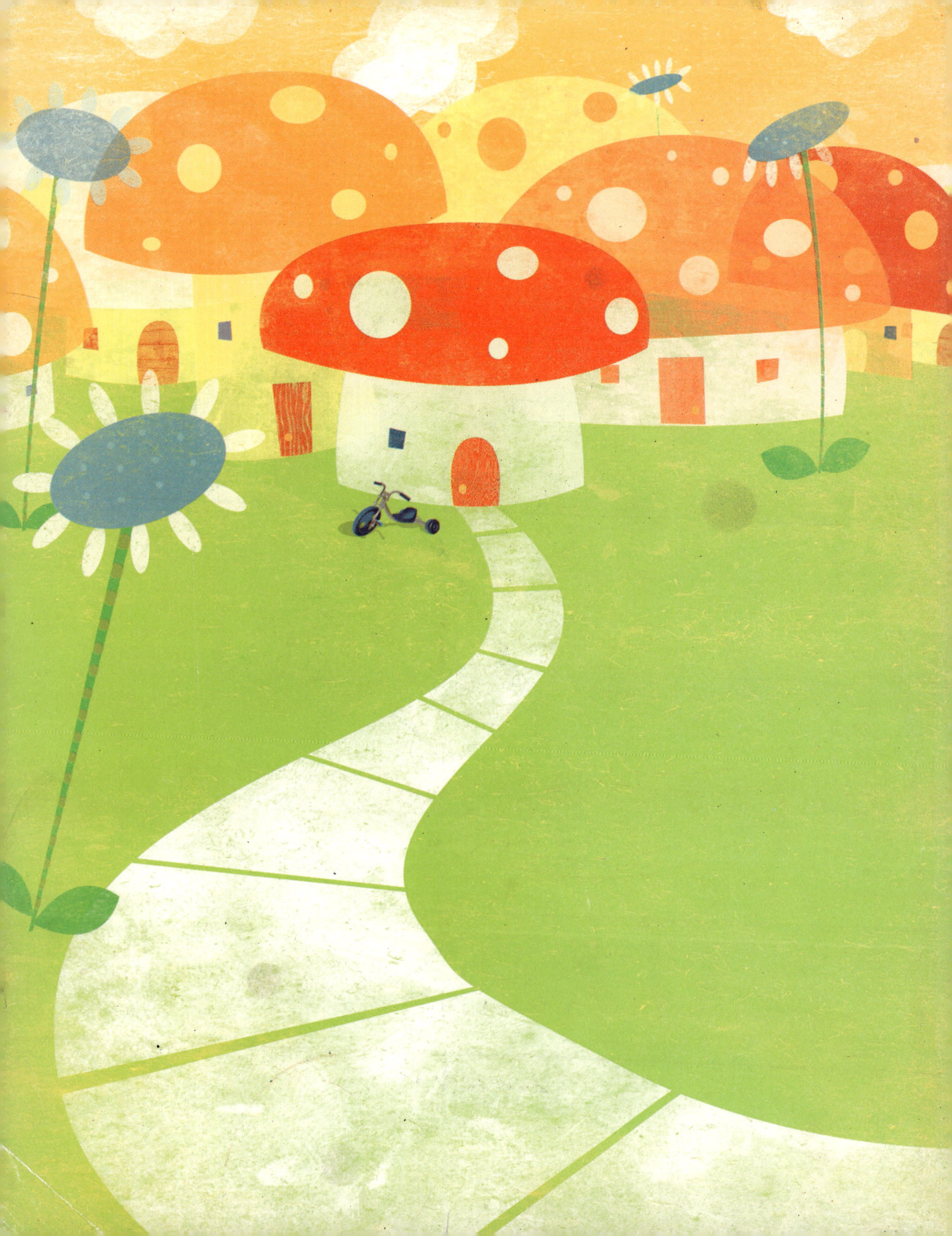

Oh, the doors you will open!